MW01620644

Christmas Wishes

Christmas Wishes

A Catalog of Vintage Holiday Treats and Treasures

Tim Hollis

STACKPOLE BOOKS

Published by
STACKPOLE BOOKS
5067 Ritter Road
Mechanicsburg, PA 17055
www.stackpolebooks.com

Printed in China

10 9 8 7 6 5 4 3 2 1

FIRST EDITION

Library of Congress Cataloging-in-Publication Data

Hollis, Tim.
Christmas wishes : a catalog of vintage holiday treats and treasures / Tim Hollis. — 1st ed.
p. cm.
Includes bibliographical references.
ISBN-13: 978-0-8117-0507-3 (hardcover)
ISBN-10: 0-8117-0507-2 (hardcover)
1. Christmas—United States—History—20th century. 2. Toys—United States—History—20th century. 3. Gifts—United States—History—20th century. I. Title.
GT4985.H573 2010
394.2663—dc22

2009051984

Contents

139

Introduction

EVERYONE'S A CHILD AT Christmas

Christmas was always a big event at our house, which may seem a bit strange when you learn what an unusual family I had. The stock image of Christmas Day is one with all of the kids romping down the stairs in their striped pajamas, the younger ones with feet in their sleepwear, to rip open the brightly colored packages under the tree. Then the whole extended family gathers around a huge dinner table that groans under the weight of a Christmas dinner fit for a medieval king.

Well, things weren't quite that way at my home.

To begin with, I was an only child, so if any romping around the Christmas tree were going to be done, it was my responsibility to do it, as my parents looked on. In the afternoon, when we traveled to my grandmother's house for dinner—an epic journey of about 20 feet, since she lived next door—and at the peak of our extended family, there were all of eight people around the table. Some of the older family members started dying off by the time I was four years old, so Christmas dinners became simpler and simpler, with smaller and smaller tables, as the years passed.

Nonetheless, my parents—especially my dad—were crazy over Christmas, beginning even before I was old enough to fully appreciate it. My dad, who was a junior high school English teacher, kept a journal of my activities for the first six years of my life. Somewhat unusually, he wrote these journals in the first person, as if I were the one doing the speaking. Perhaps he had an inkling that I would grow up to write about my life and experiences. From that journal of my first Christmas, in 1963, here is what he (speaking as me) wrote:

"I was nine and a half months old when my first Christmas came. I sat in Santa Claus's lap at G-E-S and pulled his whiskers."

I should probably interrupt him here to explain that G-E-S was a large discount department store here in Birmingham, Alabama, much like today's Sam's Club, in that one had to have a membership card to shop there. G-E-S also had outlets in Ohio and Missouri, and in some other states it went under the names of G-E-X or G-E-M. Now, back to Dad's journal:

Yep, this is me on my first Christmas. It would appear that I have that particular Santa Claus in a rather delicate predicament. Ho ho OH, right?

"I was extremely excited over the lights for the Christmas tree. Also, I was so thrilled over the live Christmas tree. I even cried when Daddy had to carry the tree back into the yard to cut it off because it was too tall.

"I received many toys. Among them was a wind-up train; horse on rollers; two telephones; turtle on a string; and a pounding board. Some clothes were also among my gifts."

For the next six years, he kept a thorough, ongoing list of what I got each year. In 1964, my biggest present was one of those horses on springs that had taken the place of the formerly reliable old rocking horses. I immediately named mine Alfred, after the main character in a Whitman Tell-a-Tale book, *The Pony That Couldn't Say Neigh*, which had quickly become my favorite story. Looking back at it now, the story follows much the same pattern as *Dumbo* or *Rudolph the Red-Nosed Reindeer* or any number of other tales wherein the hero's seeming disability or handicap turns out to be his crowning glory. I think the reason the story of Alfred appealed to me so much, even at a year-and-a-half old, was that the title character did not end up using his unique abilities to save his fellow barnyard denizens or make better friends with them, but to succeed on his own merits and leave the rest of them behind him in the dust. A psychiatrist probably could read a lot into my love for that story.

Now it's 1964, and for my second Christmas, I'm getting the horse on springs, which I named Alfred. This was also our first artificial tree; notice the foil light reflectors in the shapes of stars.

My dad's journal entry for 1965 gives only the slightest hint that we had just moved into a new house, which was built on the same spot as the house where I had spent my first two Christmases. This house is now the museum I live in today. Dad wrote:

"I got up at 8 o'clock and went down the stairs and peeked into the den to see what Santa Claus had left under the tree. [Our previous house had neither stairs nor a den.] He left a fire engine I could ride in; a blackboard; a wagon; Building Boulders [which you may recall as a tie-in with *The Flintstones*]; wind-up giraffe [which scared me half out of my wits—maybe that's why I'm a halfwit today]; puzzles; and some 'blown-up' toys."

After 1965, he dispensed with the narrative and simply listed the toys I received. The names of some of them will probably sound familiar to some of you as well. In 1966, I received a *Romper Room* tricycle with a figure of mascot Mister Do Bee mounted on the front; when a button was pressed, he would spout various prosocial phrases, such as "Did you drink your milk?" Mister Do Bee was not the only talking toy I received that year; I also was given one of Mattel's long-marketed Bugs Bunny dolls. Staying within the cartoon realm, I got a Kenner Change-A-Channel TV Set, which was a miniature movie projector that showed 8-millimeter silent films on its screen. Other gifts were an electric train and a set of ABC blocks, which I usually used to construct replicas of stores such as Woolworth's and W. T. Grant, using the blocks to carefully spell out the sign on the front of each. Some people are of the opinion that I was a rather different sort of kid—you think?

Here we are in 1966, in the house my parents built the year before. Yes, I still have this tree and 90 percent of the original decorations, but I no longer have that Yogi Bear shirt I'm wearing. Not keeping it was a big boo-boo.

Not only are the toys I got in 1968 memorable—notice the Lite-Brite—but these days you won't often see the type of rope garland that is on that tree.

The lists grew longer for each succeeding year and included many toys that are now in my above-mentioned museum. How many of you remember Hasbro's talking Snow White telephone, where a spin of the dial could connect you with Snow herself or any of her seven vertically challenged companions? Mattel brought out its own version, the Mattel-O-Phone, where you could hear short renditions of Peanuts comic strip

By 1971, the old rope garland had been replaced by more standard tinsel, but it was the same tree. I think every single toy in this photo still resides in the museum in which I live.

episodes over the receiver. I had them both at one time or another. There was Remco's battery-operated robot version of the Tin Man from *The Wizard of Oz*, and a Mickey Mouse watch in the days when it was no longer considered "cool" to have Mickey's picture on the dial; only his name was printed there to keep the tradition alive. In 1968, I got a new record player to replace the one I had been using for years; this model was the first I ever had that would play LPs in addition to 45s and 78s.

As we move through the pages that follow, each one seeming to bring back more memories than the previous page, you will no doubt catch me doing some more reminiscing about the highly personal role some of these Christmas traditions played in my life. Since I am the last surviving member of the family, with no heirs, these memories have taken on a meaning they could not possibly have had before. When I go, they will go with me, and that will be the end of them. It is my sincere hope, as well as that of my publisher, that you will be able to rekindle your own warm, fuzzy feelings and pass them along to your loved ones. And a Merry Christmas to everyone, everywhere!

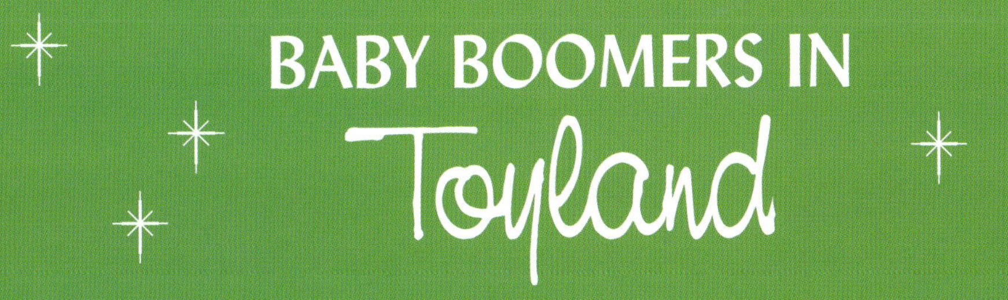

BABY BOOMERS IN Toyland

CHAPTER 1

This question is for all of you baby boomers who are standing by to dive into the rest of this book and wallow around in Christmas nostalgia until you are weeping with pure joy. Ready for it? Okay, here goes: When you think back to your childhood, and Christmas was drawing closer and closer with each day marked off the calendar, what was the first thing on your mind? Just like the teachers we used to watch on *Romper Room*, I can hear your answer right now. Here it comes:

"TOOOOOYYYYSSSS!!!!"

Very good, students. Yes, while Christmas meant many other things, both spiritual and material, when you were a kid, admit it—it was the thought of getting all those things you ever wanted, and never needed, that kept you busy marking pages in the Sears catalog and prevented you from going to sleep on Christmas Eve. Toys were available the rest of year, for birthdays and other such special occasions, but none of those events produced the overflowing cornucopia that could be found under nearly any middle-class Christmas tree on the morning of December 25.

We all grew up at a most opportune time in American history. It was the soldiers returning home after World War II that began the baby boom in 1946, and psychologists and physicians referred to the first wave as the "welcome home" babies. Unlike past similar events, though, this time it did not slow down after the first nine months. Postwar prosperity had created a nation where people could, for the first time, truly indulge and spoil their children with oodles of toys in neat suburban neighborhoods, in homes that looked like the one in which the Brady Bunch lived, providing plenty of room to play. Dads worked and moms stayed home, and all seemed right with the world. The

Santa has just opened the doors of
WOOLWORTH'S
wonderland of
TOYS
AUTHENTIC MODEL KITS!
These scale models by Revell are easy-to-assemble . . . no sanding or cutting. A wonderful hobby for Son and Dad . . . fun, educational!
B-36 BOMBER. It's the world's largest combat aircraft! 15" wingspan. Display stand. 98c
'PEACEMAKER' COLT REVOLVER . . . named by Wild Bill Hickok. 45 cal. 6-shots. 11" long. Display stand. 98c
B-52 BOMBER. Boeing Stratofortress, the heaviest military plane built to date. On display stand. 98c
SIKORSKY HELICOPTER. Used by all the Armed Services. Exact reproduction with 13" rotor. 89c
S. S. UNITED STATES. The world's fastest luxury liner. Full-color reproduction, 21" long. 1.98
PT BOAT. "Hero" of the Philippines in World War II. Full crew and armament. 9" long. 89c
By Revell
A WHOLE WONDERLAND OF TOYS . . . from cuddly animals for the girls to "make-believe" mechanical replicas for the boys! See the big selection *today* at Woolworth's . . . you can do all your toy shopping in one trip.
A. "PAJAMA POOCH," zip pouch. 4.95
B. FRENCH POODLE, soft, floppy body! 2.98
By Gloria Toy Co., Inc.
C. FLOPPY-EARED DOG that squeaks! 1.98
LIONS, TIGERS, other animals. Ea. 2.98
By R & R Toy Mfg. Co.
D. PLUSH KEWPEE DOLL and PLUSH SANTA with stuffed bodies, vinyl heads. Ea. 2.98
By Knickerbocker Toy Co.
E. BOUNCY RUBBER BALLS. 25c to 79c
By Eagle Rubber Co., Inc.
F. ANIMAL FARM SET. 20 pieces. 79c
G. SUPER RACER with silvery trim. 69c
H. TRACTOR AND WAGON. 79c
I. HORSESHOE SET. 98c
By Auburn Rubber Co., Inc.
J. HYDRAULIC LIFT DUMP TRUCK that really works. 5.69
By Structo Mfg. Co.
K. SKIPPY THE TRICKY CYCLIST pedals 'round and 'round! Loads of fun! 69c
By Craig Stanton & Co.
L. COFFEE POT AND PERCOLATOR SETS. Service for 2 or 4! 89c to 1.89
By Aluminum Specialty Co.
M. "BIG NOISE" Deluxe Training Rifle. 2.98
By Daisy Mfg. Co.
REALISTIC METAL TOYS THAT REALLY WORK—
It's such fun to play with toys like these that *do* things! The tractor steers, lifts and dumps . . . the shovel-truck's cab revolves . . . the fire engine's ladders hook together or swivel. See them all, and put plenty on your list . . . for joyous shouts Christmas morning.
BIG TRACTOR-LOADER. 2.89
THUNDERBIRD SPORTSCAR. 1.49
SHOVEL-TRUCK revolves! 1.89
LUMBER TRUCK with detachable cab, trailer. 1.89
HOOK 'N' LADDER TRUCK. 98c
by HUBLEY MFG. CO.
FUN FOR EVERYONE FROM WOOLWORTH'S!
A locomotive that's big enough for a tot to ride . . . a doll that walks . . . gay Disney puppets and blocks . . . and much, much more! All these toys are terrific *values* . . . they're all at Woolworth's, and they're all wonderful!
A. "Lightning Express" Ride-Er Locomotive. 4.95
B. Friction-Siren Fire Truck. 1.98
C. Four-Unit Sparkling Freight Train Set, with tracks. 2.89
D. Disneyland Blocks. 49c
E. Mickey Mouse, Pluto puppets. 98c
F. "Susan Stroller" Doll. 7.95
G. Doll dresses, coats, hats. 69c to 1.98
(Some prices on these pages slightly higher in West and Canada.)
At Most Woolworth Stores
Shop your Woolworth store first
F. W. WOOLWORTH CO.
IN CANADA, TOO . . . Canadian-made merchandise . . . some differences from this page, but the same wonderful toy values!
Ask for your free copy of "GIFTS AND TOYS FROM WOOLWORTH'S" at any Woolworth store. It's a wonderfully helpful Christmas shopping guide!
Listen to THE WOOLWORTH HOUR! A full hour of "What's New in Music," Sunday afternoon, CBS Radio.

prosperity slowly ground to a halt in the 1970s, but by then even the youngest baby boomers had reached their teenage years, and there were fewer kids coming up behind us to really notice the difference.

In this chapter, I am not going to be talking about the histories behind the creation of our favorite toys. Those stories, fascinating as they are, have been related in many other books and television documentaries already. No, I am simply going to give an overview of some of the main genres of toys most of us received for Christmas at one time or another. If your particular prized possession is not mentioned, it is certainly not because no one cares about it; there just isn't room for everything that could be found on those well-stocked department and variety store shelves of the 1950s through the early 1970s.

Now, if you were a girl, it's likely that at some point you wanted a doll. Ah, but the question then became what *kind* of doll? There were the traditional baby dolls, which sometimes did nothing but open and close their eyes, but more often wet their pants frequently, such as the immortal Betsy Wetsy. Bob Hope once made reference to a doll—that actually was marketed—that got diaper rash. "It comes with a bottle of liquid you pour on the rash and it disappears," Hope deadpanned. "They oughta try it on the guy who thought it up."

There were talking dolls, including Mattel's Chatty Cathy. Randi Reader talked "for a full seven minutes," according to the ads, no doubt leading some kids to invent creatively violent ways to shut her up. Little Miss Echo contained a hidden tape recorder, so as to play back whatever was just said to her. One can easily imagine little brothers causing Little Miss Echo to make all manner of ill-mannered remarks to her owner. Ideal Toys made kissing the main feature of its Kissy dolls, which puckered their lips when their arms were moved. For those who thought dolls had already done everything, the 1963 Sears catalog offered a doll identified only as Dr. Ben Casey's Patient. The accident-prone plaything came with arm and leg casts, crutches, candy pills, bandages, and Band-Aids. I kid you not.

Mattel made all the other dolls hang their heads in embarrassment when that idealized teenager Barbie made her debut in 1959. Sooner than you could say "checking account," Barbie was joined on the shelves—and in little girls' toy rooms—by so many family members and friends that it would take a genealogist to keep up with them all. There was longtime second-banana boyfriend, Ken, along with Barbie's best friend, Midge; her less-than-best friends Francie, Stacey, and Christie (who coincidentally happened to wear the same size clothes as Barbie); her kid sister, Skipper; and Skipper's friends Ricky and Skooter—and that does not even include Ken's circle of brawny buddies.

Some parents felt that Barbie's sexy look, which obviously had helped her make

As a kid, I always wanted to build my own amusement park in the backyard. Since that wasn't practical, I ended up getting one of these Child Guidance Kiddie Land sets for Christmas 1967.

This was just a small portion of Mattel's vast doll line in 1967. Look closely, ladies, and you just might see one of your own cuddly childhood play pals!

friends and influence people beyond what was considered to be healthy, was eroding good old American ideals—so in 1962, Ideal answered with the Tammy doll, a sweet, wholesome little teenager instead of a conniving fashion plate like Barbie. She came with her own crowd, but instead of rockin' and rollin' teenyboppers, Tammy was joined by a respectable Mom and Dad (you'd never catch Barbie hanging with her parents!), brother Ted, and sister Pepper. Sears very cagily stayed above the fray, selling a dollhouse that it frankly advertised would fit either Barbie or Tammy. Smart chaps, those guys at Sears.

By the late 1960s, like much of the rest of society, dolls started to get a little weird. Unlikely as it seems, much of their newfound funkiness came from Barbie's home turf, Mattel. The company had already started

Above left: ***Barbie was beside herself—and Ken and Midge were beside her, too—in this ad from 1963.*** **Below left:** ***By 1967, Barbie's circle of friends and relations was growing, and so were her career ambitions. Montgomery Ward allied itself with Braniff Airlines to employ Barbie as a stewardess.*** **Below:** ***Mattel's Liddle Kiddles were not overly strange, except for their outsize, staring eyes. Their big selling point was their tiny size, which encouraged kids—and their parents—to buy more and more of them.***

the only slightly bizarre Liddle Kiddles and followed them up with Skediddlers. The latter had moving legs that appeared to walk when pushed along by a stick in the figures' back. Skediddlers came in the shapes of various cartoon characters, most notably the Disney crew and the Peanuts cast. However, no Mattel product could fit the "anti-Barbie" mold as well as the short-lived Upsies and Downsies.

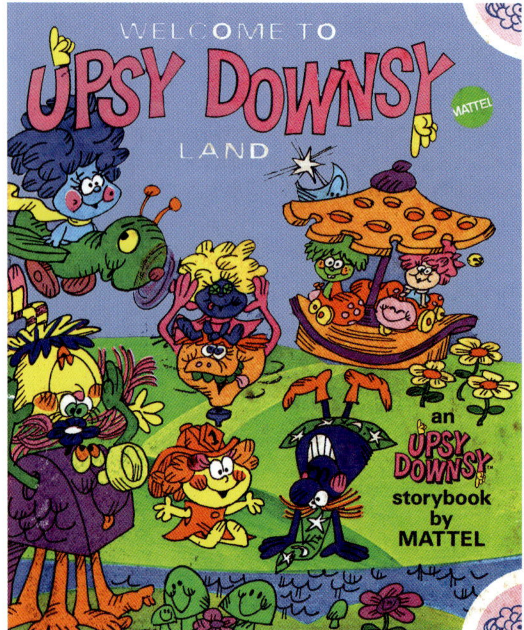

One of the weirdest concepts to hit the doll industry was Upsy Downsy Land, with its groovy Day-Glo colors and psychedelic characters.

Don't look at me that way; I'm telling the truth here. In 1969, Mattel introduced the weird world of Upsy Downsy Land, where half the population walked normally (the Upsies), and the other half walked on its hands, with feet waving in the air (the Downsies, natch). Realizing that the whole concept might be a bit weak, Mattel rolled out the secret weapon of molding the figures, and their various accessories, in blindingly loud Day-Glo colors. These made the toys fairly leap out from their surroundings on toy shelves, but did not ensure success. After only a short time, the Upsies and Downsies were sent back to whatever magical realm had spawned them, as if they had been part of a bad drug trip. (Considering the psychedelic trappings of Upsy Downsy Land, and the era in which it appeared, it is impossible not to think that Mattel's designers had the nicknames "uppers" and "downers" somewhere in the backs of their minds.)

Now for a statement that may well rock the foundations of the world: Boys played with dolls too. Oh yes, they did—only the toy makers were intelligent enough to not refer to them by that name. In 1964, Hasbro blew reveille on its bugle and rolled out G.I. Joe, who was really nothing more than a rough and tough counterpart to Barbie and her many different outfits and accessories. The jingle in the TV commercials was set to the tune of "The Caissons Go Rolling Along": "G.I. Joe, G.I. Joe, fighting man from head to toe . . ." Since no one wanted to admit that Joe was a doll, the term "action figure" was born out of the necessity of some way to describe him.

G.I. Joe came with outfits representing every branch of the military and then some, and equipment ranging from jeeps to canteens to implements of warfare. That caused a bit of a problem as the 1960s wore on and people began to get sick and tired of the real-life war in Vietnam that was being played out on the TV screens daily. G.I. Joe was no longer the heroic figure he started out to be, and in the 1970s he was converted into a more action-adventure style character. Instead of waging war, he participated in archaeological digs and such. In the 1980s, his warlike personality returned, and he was given a whole set of patriotic companions with whom to share his violent adventures, but by then his team could easily be lost among the crowd of imitators that had muscled their way into his territory—Transformers, He-Man, and on and on.

Although model kits were not an exclusively male phenomenon, they were most commonly constructed by males. Aurora was the leader when it came to models, which the company referred to as "hobby kits," and produced everything from airplanes to sailing ships to replicas of famous movie and television characters and their accompanying vehicles. One of Aurora's best-selling lines was its Prehistoric Scenes, capitalizing on the long-established love affair between kids and dinosaurs. Aurora

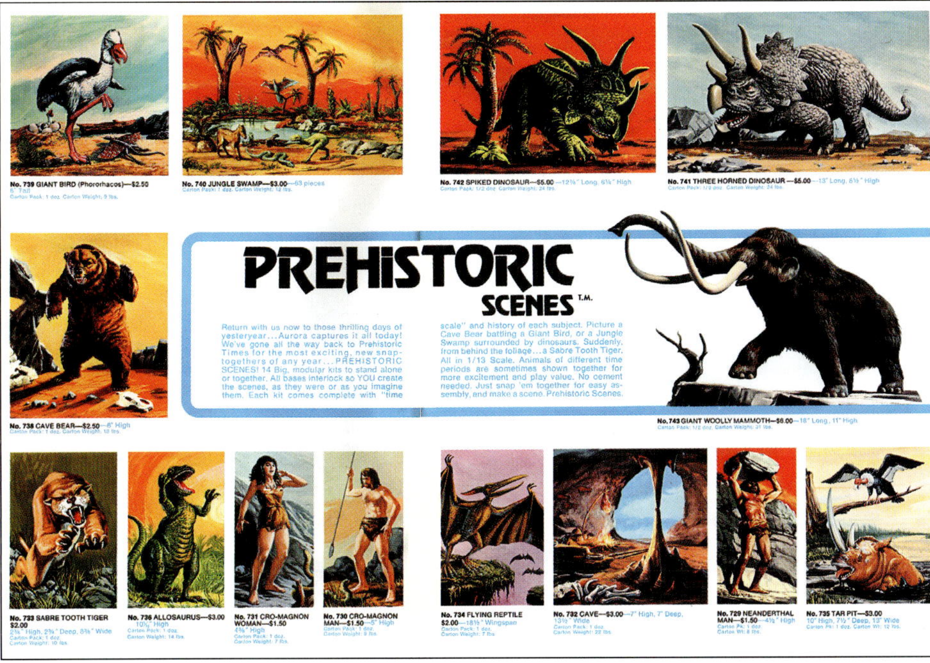

Magnon woman, for example, was a total babe in her brief, Raquel Welch–style outfit, but she was modeled recoiling in horror from a totally fictitious two-headed snake. With critters like that lurking about, no wonder they had so much trouble in the Garden of Eden.

Aurora did not have to be concerned with historical or biological accuracy when it came to its best-remembered series of model kits, the Classic Movie Monsters

When Aurora was not digging up prehistoric beasts for its model kits, it was resurrecting the living dead for its models of famous monsters of filmland. Each one had certain parts—easy to discern here—that glowed in the dark.

Aurora's Prehistoric Scenes model kits were the joy of many junior dinosaur buffs. And speaking of buff, take a peek at the sexy Cro-Magnon Woman in the bottom row. Yabba dabba doo!

did not limit its antediluvian animals to sauropods, though. Many others, from a woolly mammoth to a giant bird, stamped across the plastic landscape.

The fine print in Aurora's advertising cannily stated that at times, animals from different time periods would sometimes be depicted together for "more excitement and play value." They did not address the occasional appearance of beasts that never existed at all. Aurora's version of a Crolineup. Originally marketed in the early 1960s, the undead cast was resurrected in the latter part of the decade and given certain parts that glowed in the dark. As the series title suggested, most of the figures were replicas of the creepy creeps brought to life on the silver screen: Universal's Frankenstein monster, Dracula, the Creature from the Black Lagoon, the Mummy, the Phantom of the Opera, and other horrors. The vaults of other movie studios were raided for Godzilla and King Kong, and there were even a few creatures of non-movie origin, including a witch and the skeletal remains of the Forgotten Prisoner. As out of place as these might have seemed under a Christmas tree, they were in high demand at the time, and judging from the prices for which they sell on the collectors' market, they are in even greater demand forty years later.

Other than dolls and kid warfare, the vast majority of toys that could be found on shelves and under Christmas trees were unisex, equally appealing to both boys and girls. Board games were always popular sellers, some of them sticking around for several generations. Who doesn't remember

Parker Brothers had some of the most famous, and also some of the most forgotten, games in toy history. If you didn't have Monopoly or Clue, chances were that one of your friends did.

Candy Land, with its illustrated board that looked good enough to eat? Just the paintings of the Peanut Brittle House, Gumdrop Mountains, and Ice Cream Floes were enough to set the players to drooling in earnest. A different type of drooling for an older crowd was produced by Twister, which encouraged players of the opposite sex to entangle their bodies in creative configurations as they strained to reach the required colored polka dots.

Even in the world of games, there were occasional clearly drawn lines of demarcation: Mystery Date was the quintessential girls' game, preparing young ladies for the true game of Russian roulette they would be playing when seeking out a real-life suitor. The commercials showed adolescents giggling over the game, while a lounge singer performed the jingle: "Mystery Date, are you ready for your Mystery Date? / Don't be late, it might be great / Open the door to your [GIRL: Sigh] Mystery Date!"

There was an important sub-genre of games that, like Aurora's monster models, appealed to those kids who enjoyed scaring themselves out of seven years' growth. The

Hasbro had a hit with Mr. Potato Head and his family in the early 1950s. Many people have forgotten that for years, the facial and body parts did not come with a plastic potato, forcing us to steal spuds from Mom's vegetable drawer in the refrigerator.

Transogram toy company's Green Ghost and Ka-Bala games were meant to be played in the dark, and there were any number of other variations on the horror theme, including Which Witch and Mystic Skull, "the game of voodoo." Any of these games could be counted on to provide at least synthetic creeps, while those girls who were busy playing Mystery Date had to contend with the genuine creep who might be behind the secret door.

Boys and girls alike could become junior mad doctors with the Operation game, using tweezers to remove the various diseased organs of patient Cavity Sam. While prying for Sam's "wrenched ankle" (a monkey wrench), "water on the knee" (a bucket) or "writer's cramp" (a pencil), if the tweezers touched the surrounding metal edge, Sam's red lightbulb nose lit up and an alarm buzzer sounded. An even more morbid pastime could be enjoyed with Clue, which gave players a chance to solve a murder: "It was Colonel Mustard in the kitchen with a candlestick."

Games based on licensed characters were popular as long as their namesake figure remained in the public eye. One of the longest running was Uncle Wiggily, based on the seemingly endless series of short stories by Howard R. Garis. The Uncle Wiggily game has been on the market continuously in one form or another for so many years that most people who are familiar with it today have no idea it originated in children's books. Most other character-based games experienced a season or two of popularity and were then replaced by the next crop of characters.

Character licensing was the only distinguishing feature of the many different types of plastic punching bags, or Punch-Me's, that allowed kids to work out their frustrations by hitting something other than their younger siblings. Each figure had a weighted bottom so it would bounce back up after a hard punch. The odd thing about these toys was that for the most part, the characters chosen to be depicted on them were hardly

Punching bags came in the shape of every conceivable cartoon star. The odd thing about this 1971 lineup is that not a single one of them was the type of character any normal kid would want to punch in the snoot.

the type to normally inspire violence. What sick kid would have any desire to whale away at such comical friends as Yogi Bear, Bozo the Clown, Fred Flintstone, Woody Woodpecker, Mister Magoo, or (heavens to animal cruelty!) Flipper? And let's face it—any kid needed to be placed under psychiatric watch if he deliberately chose to punch Superman, Batman, or Popeye. For a truly disturbing concept, none of the other punching bags could approach a generic character called Scatter Brain, the top of whose head was a transparent container filled with colored balls. Hitting this mug in the mug would cause his "brains" to rattle and bounce.

Not all kids had an insatiable urge to hit something, and for those of a more creative bent, there were toys that appealed to their inner (or outer) artist. Old standbys such as paint-by-number sets were joined by Kenner's Sparkle Paints (which were definitely a joy to all parents when the necessary glitter ended up embedded in the shag carpeting) and Hasbro's Stardust Velvet Art. Silly Sand, which took messy art to a new level, was another way for kids to express themselves. Then there was Lite-Brite, with a bulb behind a screen that illuminated colorful pegs as they were pushed through the required holes. As with almost any other toy, once Lite-Brite had established itself, it began mutating into new forms. There was a "moving" version with two levels of pegs instead of just one, so that moving them

This is the same Lite-Brite you saw under my tree in one of the photos in this book's Introduction. You may be able to make out an actual 1970 Christmas seal glued in the center of the box.

back and forth made the peg figures appear to move in the manner of neon signage. Before it was over, Lite-Brite had come out with additional refill pages featuring Bozo the Clown, Bugs Bunny and his looney pals, and the Peanuts gang.

Now let's turn our eyeballs to a classification that could probably be called "optical toys." The oldest and most durable of these was the View-Master, which had been around since the late 1930s but became a true toy super-seller during the baby boom years. Stereopticon photos were nothing new; even as far back as the turn of the century, many households had viewers and their flat cards, with two photos shot from slightly different angles, as a parlor diversion. The View-Master put the scenes into reels, in vivid color, so that peering through the viewer gave them startling depth and the type of luminosity that could usually be seen only by watching a motion picture on a big screen.

View-Master made much of its income by producing reels (and soon, packages of three reels totaling twenty-one scenes) for tourist attractions, where they were always popular souvenir shop items. Where the company really took off, though, was when it bought out a smaller stereopticon company known as Tru-Vue in 1951. That company had been doing basically the same thing, but its slides were elongated cards rather than reels. Tru-Vue's ace in the hole was that it held the license to produce scenes from the Disney movies, and once View-Master inherited those rights, the television- and cartoon-based reels and packets knew no bounds. The company kept marketing reels (as View-Master) and cards (as Tru-Vue) well into the 1960s, when the cards were finally discontinued.

The Kenner company got the prize for the most variations on the optical toy theme. It began with the Give-A-Show projector in 1960. Most baby boomers had at

The number of different subjects available as View-Master reels really made the mind reel. These are just a few, ranging from Disney films to Hanna-Barbera characters to famous tourist attractions.

Each Set with 6 exciting movies of TV favorites

No. 774—**Super Heroes Set. Pkd. $\frac{1}{2}$ doz., wt. $12\frac{3}{4}$ lbs.**

No. 772/773 ASSORTMENT **pkd. $\frac{1}{2}$ doz., wt. $12\frac{3}{4}$ lbs.** Sets feature Yogi Bear, Huck Hound, Superman, Bugs Bunny, others.

No. 7809

EXTRA SETS OF MOVIES (TWO DISPLAY ASSORTMENTS)

Movies of Dick Tracy, Three Stooges, Lassie, The Munsters, Mr. Magoo, and many others.

No. 7809—**4 doz. Display Asst., wt. $5\frac{3}{4}$ lbs.** No. 7808—**2 doz. Display Asst., wt. 3 lbs.**

GIVE-A-SHOW PROJECTORS

and extra sets of shows.

Giant-size, bright color pictures up to 8 ft. by 8 ft. 16 shows of TV stars, 112 color slides. Uses 3 size "D" batteries not included.

No. 508—**pkd. $\frac{1}{2}$ doz., wt. 10 lbs.**

No. 507—**pkd. $\frac{1}{2}$ doz., wt. 10 lbs.**

TWO FLOOR DISPLAY RACKS

No. 5071—**1 doz. No. 507's, wt. 22 lbs.**

No. 5081—**1 doz. No. 508's, wt. 22 lbs.**

Counter Display Asst. of Additional Shows No. 120, 2 doz., wt. $6\frac{1}{4}$ lbs. 24 sets, 6 different shows to set

Kenner's Give-A-Show Projector, with its rows of slides, and Easy-Show Projector, which ran 8-millimeter films, turned kids everywhere into would-be theater impresarios.

Kenner's®

SEE-A-SHOW

stereo viewer sets

No. 103 ASSORTMENT. Pkd. 2 doz., wt. 7 lbs. 3 sets, each with 35 stereo scenes, of 5 shows that feature the Super Heroes, King Kong, Mr. Magoo, and others. Equally assorted.

No. 103-6 DUMP DISPLAY ASSORTMENT SEE-A-SHOW SETS, wt. 19¼ lbs. 6 doz. equally assorted of the 3 sets in 103 Asst. Pkd. in display—ready to use.

No. 203 SEE-A-SHOW STEREO VIEWER SET, pkd. 1 doz., wt. 5¾ lbs.

The See-A-Show was Kenner's stereopticon answer to the much more successful View-Master series.

least one example of this toy, which was reissued in a new edition each year. The battery-operated projector was not much more than a glorified flashlight, with color slides of various television and cartoon favorites. (It must have been frustrating to Kenner to have the rights to practically every cast of characters in the media, from the Looney Tunes bunch to Captain Kangaroo to the Hanna-Barbera menagerie, but *not* any properties from the wonderful world of Disney.) Like the View-Master reels, a Give-A-Show Projector story was told in seven frames, usually with dialogue indicated in captions at the bottom of each picture.

Kenner realized that still images had only limited entertainment value, so the logical next step was the Easy-Show Movie Projector. Now, instead of strips of slides, the projector came with actual silent 8-millimeter films of the cartoon stars. The trade-off for this increased potential was that the films had to be in black and white rather than in color. It is safe to say that many children got their first exposure to the true nature of animation, and motion pictures in general, by studying the frame-by-frame progression of the action in these toy films. The Easy-Show films came with two separate features on each reel, pairing Bozo the Clown with Casper the Friendly Ghost, or Lassie with Porky Pig, for example.

The Easy-Show Projector then doubled the fun with Kenner's Change-A-Channel TV Set. Now the projection mechanism was housed in a miniature boob tube, and the films came with four features per reel, two of which were printed side-by-side on the film stock. By flipping the channel dial, kids could switch back and forth between the two simultaneously playing cartoons. As a kid, I wondered why they didn't go ahead and throw in commercials too, since it was supposed to be so much like watching television. Kenner even had its own lower-tech version of the View-Master with its See-A-Show viewer. It harked back to the earliest days of stereopticon photography in that the scenes were printed on card stock instead of film. The effect was not all that great, but quite a few cartoon characters made it into See-A-Show slides who never graduated to the Give-A-Show format.

Having already gummed up the works with Gloppy, Kenner introduced the phosphorescent Glow-Globs, which, as you can see from this ad, dispensed with jolly character molds and tried to be spooky instead.

***Kenner's Gloppy, a clone of Play-Doh, came packaged in molds shaped like Hanna-Barbera cartoon superstars Yogi Bear and Fred Flintstone, and not-quite-a-star Gloop, one of the weird cast members of* The Herculoids.**

Actually, Kenner was pretty good at coming up with clones of other companies' successful toys. We all know about Play-Doh, that colorful putty with the distinctive smell that was good for modeling figures and abstract shapes (and if what you were molding didn't come out looking like you'd planned, you could always claim it was the latter). But how many of you remember Kenner's version of Play-Doh, known as Gloppy? Not many, huh? Gloppy did not stay on the market for long, and what attention it did attract was due to the fact that it came packaged in molds shaped like popular Hanna-Barbera cartoon stars. There was also a Circus Gloppy set, but if Secret

Squirrel and Fred Flintstone couldn't move the stuff, a generic lion and elephant didn't have much of a chance. Kenner stuck its hand in the glop again with Glow-Globs, publicized as the "weird new modeling gunk that glows in the dark." Basically a phosphorescent version of Gloppy, Glow-Globs came in molds shaped like ghosts, skeletons, and other haints.

Lest it be thought that Kenner was only good at copying others, let the record show that the company was equally talented at stealing from itself. You ladies recall playing with Kenner's Easy-Bake Oven, the aqua-colored kitchen appliance that cooked food over two 100-watt lightbulbs. Like a doll, it was one toy brothers would not go near, unless it was to eat whatever Sis had Easy-Baked up for them. But what about those boys' dads, who could be found on spring and summer evenings cooking up hamburgers on the backyard grill, with a chef's hat and "Kiss the Cook" apron to make the ensemble complete? Kenner thought about them and introduced the Easy-Bake's guy equivalent, the Big Burger Grill. It used only one lightbulb to cook the equivalent of a manly meal, but apparently boys decided it was better to leave the grilling to dear ol' Dad, since the Big Burger Grill is hardly a candidate for the Toy Hall of Fame these days.

While girls were using their Easy-Bake Ovens to cook like Mom, their brothers could emulate Dad with the Big Burger Grill. "Hold the onions, son. I got a hot date with your mama tonight."

Naturally, Kenner was not the only company to involve itself in a bit of copycatting around. For any toys that were more than moderately successful, it was likely that knock-off imitators would soon appear. Lego blocks, those plastic bricks with the many connecting teeth that could be used to build any variety of shapes, were widely copied. Lego was obviously the inspiration for Mattel's Tog'l, another variety of interlocking plastic blocks. Unlike the oblong Lego pieces, Tog'l blocks were mostly square, with occasional triangular pieces for corners. They also showed some debt to the wooden Tinkertoy sets by including green plastic tubes that could be used to connect one structure to another. During the late 1960s, Tog'l sets grew to enormous complexity, even including motors to make working models of various amusement park rides. Eventually Tog'l crashed and burned, leaving only memories and what appears to be a thriving Internet fandom among former youngsters.

Never one to let a good idea go unchallenged, Kenner's response to Lego was Flintstones Building Boulders, which were huge and made from white Styrofoam with small specks of color embedded. They did not resemble rocks nearly so much as the name implied, but like Lego and Tog'l they had interlocking teeth for constructing buildings and other imaginative structures. Through some mutually agreeable deal with Kenner, during one season of the prime-time *Flintstones* show, the opening sequence featured a brief shot of baby Pebbles playing with her Building Boulders set.

Like the Building Boulders, there are many toys that baby boomers may remember primarily from their incessant television commercials rather than from actually owning the toys. One example might be the gumball-machine banks that came in the shapes of various cartoon characters' craniums; the commercials made catchphrases of sorts out of "Penny for a gumball, Mickey!" and "Thanks for the gumball!" Besides Mickey Mouse, Popeye, Bozo the Clown, Scooby Doo, the Pink Panther, and others, the banks also came as plain plastic spheres, exciting no one's imagination.

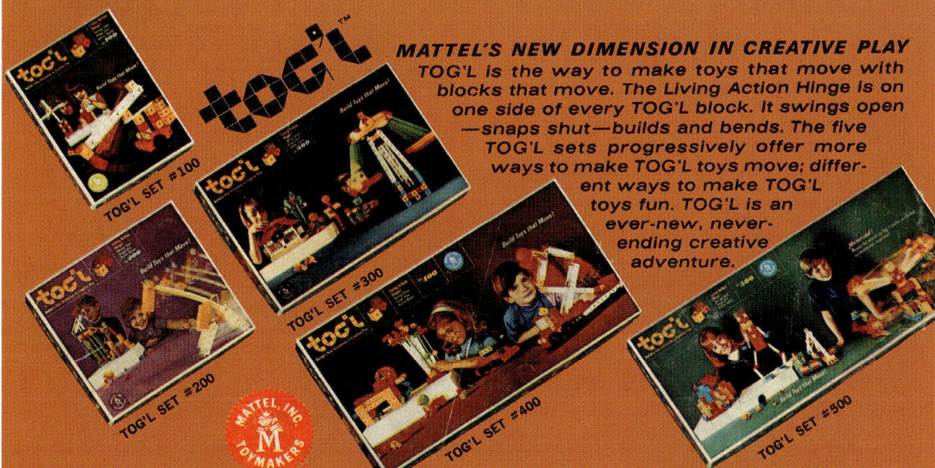

Mattel's interlocking Tog'l blocks tried to give Lego some competition but came crashing down like a quickly constructed figure. While it lasted, though, Tog'l even issued sets with motors so kids could build their own amusement park rides. The toy had been discontinued before I got old enough to have one of those advanced sets.

Unlike some other manufacturers, the Marx toy company made its commercials into a sort of unified whole, thanks to their employing the same narration style and, in most cases, the same narrator, Claude Kirchner, formerly best known as the ringmaster of the *Super Circus* series in the 1950s. After that show had folded its tent and moved on down the road, Kirchner became a local kids' show personality in New York City, but his Marx commercials were a mainstay of network television for many more years. Whether it was the remote-controlled green ghoul called the Great Garloo, the ball-spitting dragon King Zor, the Electro-Shot Shooting Gallery, Rock'Em Sock-'Em Robots, or any of their toy shelf companions, each commercial of the 1960s would somehow include Kirchner barking the name of the item, followed by the two words "BY MARX!" as loudly as possible.

Marx continued using this style into the early 1970s. Late baby boomers may well remember the constant Saturday morning commercials for the Big Wheel ("BY MARX!"), that all-plastic ride that was no more than a glorified tricycle. Its commercials generally began running about the time the new cartoon series premiered each fall, stretching all the way to Christmas. The spots seemed produced specifically for airing during that period, as they showed kids in coats and sweaters, gleefully spinning their Big Wheels' big wheels among colorful fallen leaves.

Above: ***What preschooler didn't have The Farmer Says, with the rotating hayseed pointing the way to various animal sounds? The Mattel-O-Phone came with tiny records that enabled kids to talk to various characters of legend and cartoon fame.*** **Left:** ***Nearly every city had a television station with a franchise for*** **Romper Room,** ***which came with its own heavily promoted line of toys. This version of the show was seen in Peoria, Illinois, but the same set and toys could be found on local stations from coast to coast.***

In the late 1960s, Aurora decided to move beyond the successful prehistoric and movie monster model kits cooked up by the mad geniuses at the company and enter the toy battle for real. To get the message across, Aurora brought in the proven help of the Hanna-Barbera studio, which supplied animated commercials hosted by a rather calculatedly cool rock group billed as the New Generation. Driving the slogan home, each new Aurora product was known as a "New Generation Toy," but not a single one of them stayed around long enough to become old, and Aurora soon retreated to the model kits for which it was best known. Hanna-Barbera's big toy licensee, Kenner, tagged its spots with the animated gooney bird that squawked, "It's Kenner! It's fun! Braaack!"

Several times throughout the preceding discussion, mention has been made of toys based on one famous cartoon character or another. In most cases, the characters were secondary to the toys on which their likenesses appeared. For example, the Punch-Me punching bags were basically the same, whether the image printed on them was Bullwinkle, Dennis the Menace, or Frosty the Snowman. View-Master reels and the Give-A-Show Projector licensed every character they could get their filmy paws on, yet the toy itself was the main draw. Occasionally, though, there would be such a white-hot cartoon property that the characters overshadowed the toys. One example is

Hmm, getting kids to take a bath for Christmas sounds like dirty work afoot. It was made more fun by Soaky bubble bath and its containers shaped like beloved cartoon characters. And if that failed, parents could use the Santa Soaky to remind their soiled brats that the old man was watching.

what happened with Charles Schulz's classic characters from *Peanuts*.

Even though the comic strip began in 1950, it was eight years later before any tie-in toys appeared. When they did, it was in the form of a series of hard plastic dolls, which were soon followed by coloring books that enlarged the individual panels of the comic strips to a size that could be easily worked over with crayons. Of course, most of us had at least a few (or frequently a lot) of the hardcover or paperback books that each reprinted several months' worth of the newspaper strip. The book line was expanded in 1965, when the first *Peanuts* animated television show, *A Charlie Brown Christmas*, made its debut to the accompaniment of a print adaptation. Each of the TV specials that followed also appeared in book form, but only the original and its immediate sequel, *Charlie Brown's All-Stars*, featured new artwork. No doubt because of the increased work they entailed, future books were illustrated with frame enlargements or cel setups from the actual shows.

When *Peanuts* came to television, it seems to have kick-started the merchandising campaign into high gear. By the end of

When* A Charlie Brown Christmas *kicked off the Peanuts animated TV specials in 1965, it did wonders for the infant industry of toys based on Charles Schulz's much-loved characters.

THIS CHRISTMAS CALL WARDS FOR THAT...

Talk of the Town

PEANUTS GANG!

Peanuts® Pocket® Dolls from the PEANUTS® Comic Strip by Charles M. Schulz© United Feature Syndicate, Inc. 1966 and 1967.

1-5 Good Grief—Peanuts in 3-D. Charles Schulz's lively characters are dressed just as you see them in his comic strips. About 7 in. tall, they're made of soft vinyl with movable heads, arms and legs.
(1) **48 HT 10601D**—Charlie Brown
(2) **48 HT 10605D**—Schroeder
(3) **48 HT 10604D**—Snoopy
(4) **48 HT 10603D**—Lucy
(5) **48 HT 10602D**—Linus
Ship. wt. 6 oz. each.
State cat. nos. wanted—**2.95** each;... any 2 for **5.29**;.. any 5 for **12.88**

6, 7 Happiness is being one of the gang in a sizzling orange Peanuts sweatshirt! Soft, washable cotton. Buy any 2 and save 90c.
(6) For adults. Wear Snoopy's famous statement "Curse you, Red Baron!" S(34-36 in.), M(38-40 in.), L(42-44 in.) *State size letter.*
Z48 HT 35020D—Ship. wt. 1 lb. 2 oz... each **3.95** . . . any 2 for **7.00**
(7) For children. "Happiness is having a friend." Sizes: S(size 10), M(size 12), L(size 14). Ship. wt. 1 lb. 2 oz.
Z48 HT 35022D—*State size letter.* ea. **3.95**; **2/7.00**

8-12 Security is having lots of big soft Peanuts Pillow People! They're 17 in. tall—great fun for bedrooms, rec rooms and dormitories. Plumply filled with kapok, covered with cotton muslin.
(8) **48 HT 10313D**—Snoopy
(9) **48 HT 10312D**—Schroeder
(10) **48 HT 10310D**—Linus
(11) **48 HT 10311D**—Lucy
(12) **48 HT 10309D**—Charlie Brown
Ship. wt. 14 oz. each.
State catalog numbers.......each **3.95** . . . Save 1.02—any 2 for **6.88**

13 Calendars! Choose Peanuts 1968 Date Book, or new School Year Date Book 1967–68 (not shown). The best of Peanuts comic strips on every page, big cartoon blowups, large appointment squares. School version runs from Sept. to Aug. Each 10½x13 in.
(13) **53 HT 494**—Ship. wt. 1 lb. 6 oz................Date Book **2.66**
53 HT 495—not shown. Ship. wt. 1 lb. 6 oz..........School Yr. **2.66**

14 Peanuts—the game of Charlie Brown and his pals! Whoever captures the whole Peanuts gang wins! For 2-4 players of any age.
48 HT 14214—Ship. wt. 2 lbs. 6 oz.........Complete game only **1.99**

15 Peanuts Projects! The most fun-filled activity book ever! Make Snoopy cookies! Put on the Great Pumpkin Mystery play! Crossword and jigsaw puzzles, a secret code, charades and much more to do!
53 HT 498—About 12x17 in. Ship. wt. 1 lb. 12 oz.............only **2.66**

16 Peanuts books to read again and again! All ages enjoy Charles Schulz's famous humor and priceless sentiment. Each volume has a special heart-warming theme. (01) Christmas is Together-Time; (02) Love is Walking Hand in Hand; (03) Happiness is a Warm Puppy; (04) Security is a Thumb and a Blanket; (05) I Need All the Friends I Can Get; (06) Home is on Top of a Dog House; (07) Snoopy and the Red Baron—the first full-length Peanuts novel. Ship. wt. 1 lb. 8 oz. for 2 books.
Z53 HT 489—*State title numbers*....Any 2 for **3.48** . . . Any 4 for **6.59**

17 Set of 4 books pictured for only 3.49. Here are hundreds of the best-loved Peanuts comic strips starring good old Charlie Brown.
53 HT 497—Ship. wt. 1 lb. 8 oz. ....set **3.49**

Montgomery Ward devoted a two-page spread to Peanuts merchandise in the late-1960s catalogs. If you didn't have the dolls or shirts, you probably at least had one of the many Peanuts comic strip books.

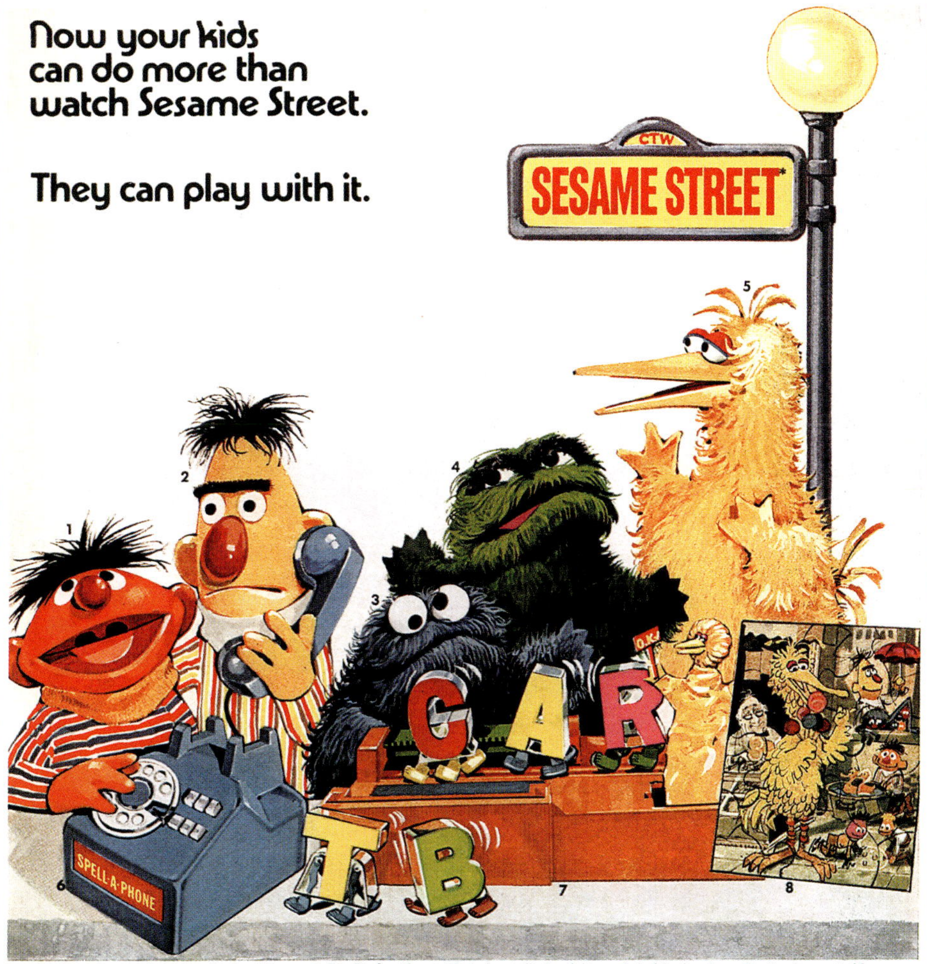

the 1960s, the characters could be found on everything from clothing to calendars to jewelry to felt pennants to stuffed toys to—well, you get the idea. Board games based on the strip were no longer the generic "whoever arrives at Point X first wins" variety. The Snoopy vs. the Red Baron game had one player impersonating the famed World War I aerial villain, dropping marbles down a chute at the other player, who stood in for heroic flying ace Snoopy. The idea was for the Snoopy player to catch the white marbles and let the blue ones pass him by.

An even more complex layout was used in Milton-Bradley's Good Ol' Charlie Brown game, where the playing board was a 3-D replica of the comic strip neighborhood. Players passed through Linus's pumpkin patch, saw Lucy's psychiatry booth and the nearby kite-eating tree, walked along the brick wall on which the characters were frequently seen leaning, and even circled around the frozen birdbath where Woodstock played ice hockey. For girls who were aspiring fussbudgets, Lucy's Tea Party had the players follow instructions for

Although* Sesame Street *debuted in November 1969, it was 1971 before any toys based on the show other than records and books were made available. Word on the street was that people might object to commercializing an educational public-television series, but the kids paid no attention to such naysayers.

pouring water into each other's teacups until one of them overflowed and made a mess—the winner!

A few years after the *Peanuts* peak, another group of characters came along that some people felt were poised to eclipse all that had come before. *Sesame Street* premiered on public television in November 1969, and merchandise began to trickle out before a year had passed, initially taking the form of books and records based on the show. From a television history standpoint, it is important to note that some of the earliest *Sesame Street* items depicted Oscar the Grouch in his original 1969–70 orange color, rather than the grungy green he would adopt ever afterward. Since Jim Henson's Muppets were a major factor in the show's success, it was not surprising that toy puppet versions of them were also a big part of the merchandise line, although it seems to have taken manufacturers a few years to realize their potential.

Uncharacteristically, the Sears Christmas catalog was loitering in the alley when *Sesame Street* hit big. It was 1972 before the tie-in items made their Sears debut—and Sears knew it had something special, because the store made a big deal out of the addition of *Sesame* items to its lineup. The original puppet line consisted of buddies Bert and Ernie, whose heads were molded out of such hard plastic that the mouths barely moved. There was also the vinyl visage of Roosevelt Franklin and fake-fur

No doubt many future Jim Hensons got their start playing with these Muppet replicas available in the early 1970s. The original hard plastic Bert and Ernie heads were later replaced by soft foam rubber, which was easier to manipulate but did not look so much like the original characters.

renditions of Oscar (by now bright green) and the Cookie Monster, who was equipped with a slit in the back of his throat so he could appear to swallow whatever was pushed into his mouth. Big Bird initially appeared as a sort of ventriloquist's figure, part stuffed toy and part hand puppet. Most of the rest of the cast joined the fun over the next few years. It is amusing to read the instructions that came on each box, as if hand puppets even needed instructions; parents were encouraged to show their children how to place a hand in the puppet to make the mouth move, and how to use a plastic wand to manipulate the character's arm. I don't know about you, but I would have to wonder about any kid who had to have someone explain how to work a hand puppet.

The *Peanuts* proliferation was one thing, but when a show that was inherently supposed to be noncommercial started filling up the toy shelves, some folks began griping that the *Sesame Street* producers were fouling their own nest. Said producers warded off such criticism by pointing out that part of the profits from licensing all those toys was going back into the production of the show. Meanwhile, the company that really seemed to resent the new kids on the street was Disney. Some felt that the *Sesame* invasion was truly meant to make kids forget about the lovable—and highly commercially successful—Disney gang. In the end, though, there seemed to be room enough for everyone. The selfsame 1972 Sears catalog that made such a big deal out of *Sesame Street*'s arrival featured the Disney Winnie the Pooh cast on the front cover and in decorative vignettes inside, so that wonderful world of color couldn't be counted out just yet.

No matter which of the many types of toys a youngster preferred—and it goes without saying that the ones discussed here do not even scratch the surface—when it came to Christmas morn, they fell into one of two categories: either they were wrapped in colorful Christmas paper, or else they were just sitting out there in the open for everyone to see. I got unwrapped presents for my first four Christmases, but after that, when I wrote my annual letter to Santa Claus, I always specifically requested that the gifts be wrapped. This produces a vivid mental image of Santa in his busy North Pole workshop, reading my letter and groaning, "Oh, no! I have to visit every kid in the world in one night, and *this* one wants me to stop and wrap every one of his dadgum toys!"

Well, for all of those others who wanted wrapped gifts too, there was seemingly no end to the available Christmas paper designs. Some were meant exclusively for children's presents, while others were more sophisticated and even expensive, such as the various styles of shiny foil paper. As beautiful as the paper was, it seemed a shame to rip it off its contents and wad it

Since many smaller stores could not afford to compile their own catalogs, they could instead send out one of these generic "Santa's Toy Books" with their own logo imprinted on the cover.

One thing that could not change too drastically over the years was Christmas gift wrap. This selection was available in 1942, and it looked practically the same three decades later.

up to be thrown out with the trash on December 26, but that was its usual fate. Occasionally one could find an economy-minded parent who insisted on removing the wrapping paper very carefully, storing it flat to remove the creases, and then reusing the same paper year after year. The manufacturers no doubt would have liked to get their fingers around the throats of such thrifty souls.

• • •

While toys were the undisputed kings of the Christmas want lists, coming in at a distant second would have to be the seemingly endless varieties of candy and other sweets that bloomed out of nowhere during the season. When Clement Clarke Moore's children were abed while visions of sugarplums danced in their heads, they were hardly the first and far from the last. A children's Christmas record of the 1960s itemized the situation thus:

> Christmas candy, Christmas candy,
> Peppermint sticks and curly-ribboned
> candy canes
> And lemon drops; chocolate Santas,
> lollipops;
> What a wonderful Christmas treat,
> All the candy that you can eat.

The uncredited lyricist for that song must have been writing it with mouth watering and stomach growling. No matter which of the yummies described in it suited one most, they could be found in riotous abundance in nearly any store of the period, from the big department stores with their

Ducky Waddles—Unusual pull toy. A metal duck, 17 in. long, that waddles along on wheels, or floats in water. Filled with 1 lb. delicious, chewy peanut butter kisses—can later be filled with sand. Ship. wt. 2 lbs.
53 T 9160—Complete......**39c**.

(A) **GOOD—Hard Candy**—All-hard asst. in variety of shapes, flavors, colors.
53 T 9000—2 lbs....**27c**
53 T 9001—5 lbs....**63c**

(B) **BETTER—Filled and Hard**—Half the pieces filled with jams, creams. Others hard.
53 T 9003—2 lbs....**33c**
53 T 9004—5 lbs....**78c**

(C) **BEST—All Filled**—Crisp, colorful sugar shells—all filled with jams, creams, nut butter, jelly.
53 T 9006—2 lbs....**35c**
53 T 9007—5 lbs....**85c**

(D) **Candy Ribbon**—Crisp hand-spun striped ribbon candy. 2-in. lengths. Ship. wt. 5 lbs.
53 T 9031—4 lbs..**$1.09**

(E) **Black Walnut Puffs** Sugar shells stuffed with chopped nut meats and cocoanut.
53 T 9036—2 lbs. ..**43c**
53 T 9037—5 lbs....**98c**

(F) **Giant Gum Drops**—Tender, sugar coated, colorful. In an assortment of true fruit flavors.
53 T 9038—2 lbs....**34c**
53 T 9039—5 lbs....**75c**

(G) **Creme Candy**—Sweet, creamy candies in a variety of flavors, shapes, colors.
53 T 9009—2 lbs....**37c**
53 T 9010—5 lbs....**85c**

(H) **Sparkling Beauty Chips**—Thin, crisp sugar wafers in assorted colors, flavors.
53 T 9237—2 lbs....**45c**
53 T 9238—5 lbs....**98c**

(J) **Peanut Brittle**—Crispy, golden-brown favorite. Full of crunchy, fresh roasted peanuts.
53 T 9012—2 lbs....**35c**
53 T 9013—5 lbs....**84c**

(K) **Chocolate Peanut Chips**—Peanut butter filling, rich chocolate coating.
53 T 9225—2 lbs....**64c**
53 T 9226—5 lbs..**$1.49**

(L) **Satin Pillows**—Shiny finish sugar shells with cocoanut or other fillings.
53 T 9015—2 lbs....**45c**
53 T 9016—5 lbs....**98c**

(M) **Almond Butter Fingers**—Slender, golden butterscotch shells stuffed with crushed almonds.
53 T 9231—2 lbs....**59c**
53 T 9232—5 lbs..**$1.39**

(N) **Cream and Gum Mix**—Assortment of fancy sugar creams and tasty jelly gums.
53 T 9024—2 lbs....**33c**
53 T 9025—5 lbs....**79c**

(P) **Midget Caramels**—Small, rich, chewy caramels covered with thick milk chocolate.
53 T 9228—2 lbs....**64c**
53 T 9229—5 lbs..**$1.59**

(R) **Festival Mix**—Assortment of fancy, fine quality hard candy—ribbon, crisp chips and wafers.
53 T 9234—2 lbs....**49c**
53 T 9235—5 lbs..**$1.15**

Shipping weights for candies above: 2-pound lot, 3 lbs.; 5-pound lot, 6 lbs.

Empty Candy Boxes—Assortment of bright colored holiday designs. Ideal for church, school, and club parties. Hold one half pound candy. Ship. wt. 8 oz.; 2 lbs. 4 oz.; 3 lbs. 11 oz.
53 T 9130—12 for............**10c**
53 T 9131—50 for............**37c**
53 T 9132—100 for...........**69c**

Christmas Stocking—Red paper or cellophane—filled with mixed hard candies. Hang on tree.
Small Stocking (1/4 lb. candy). Ship. wt. 1 lb. 2 oz.; 4 lbs.
53 T 9153—3 for............**25c**
12 Small Stockings.........**89c**
Large Stocking (1 lb. candy). Ship. wt. 1 lb. 12 oz.; 4 lbs. 12 oz.
53 T 9155—1 for............**27c**
3 large stockings..........**74c**

Blue Mints—Two-pound box of crystal-clear blue hard candy. Refreshingly cool, peppermint flavored, pure and wholesome. Each piece individually wrapped in cellophane. Packed in attractive round gift box with floral design. Ship. wt. 3 lbs.
53 T 9048—2-pound Box......**69c**

Honey Drop Cookies—Pfeffernuesse—Old-fashioned Christmas cookies—a treat for the whole family. Tasty, spicy mixture perfectly blended and baked, sweetened with honey, and covered with powdered sugar. Contains eggs, milk and other wholesome ingredients. About 150 cookies. Cellophane wrapped gift box with mailing container—ideal for a boy in the service. Ship. wt. 4 lbs. 4 oz.
53 T 9068—3½ Pounds in Box.................**95c**

158 WARDS2 B

ADD CHRISTMAS CANDY TO YOUR TIME PAYMENT ORDER—SEE PAGE 37 FOR DETAILS

Montgomery Ward presented these luscious candies in its 1942 Christmas catalog, just as wartime sugar rationing caused many of them to be unavailable. Like the gift wrap, most of these goodies were still around in the years to come.

elaborate candy counters to the small five-and-ten or variety stores.

The five-and-ten approach to Christmas candy was best exemplified by Woolworth's, although the scene was repeated at W. T. Grant, S. S. Kresge, G. C. Murphy, S. H. Kress, and any of those other chains that bore their founders' initials and last name. The main idea was for candy and a toy to be combined, usually as a molded plastic figure that held an assortment of sweets. The Woolworth's line took the form of Santa in a wagon drawn by one reindeer, a toy soldier, a miniature saxophone, and other inexpensive shapes—some holding only a few lollipops, others with copious

Woolworth's was one of the leaders in cheap plastic toys containing lollipops or bags of other types of candy, but Sears was responsible for the candy container shaped like Santa with his sleigh and all eight reindeer.

SAXOPHONE PARTY HORN
Red, yellow or green . . . with two pouches of candies and two lollipops. 9½" long.
29¢

SOLDIER AT ATTENTION!
He holds rifle and 3 pops. Yellow or white with colorful trimmings. 4" tall.
10¢

SANTA RIDES IN THE SOAP BOX DERBY!
His car's wheels turn! 8 pops. 5¼" long.
39¢

CHRISTMAS TOYS
and
DEE-LICIOUS CANDIES
all in one!

LINE UP TOY SOLDIERS...BEAT DRUMS...TOOT SAXOPHONES! ALL BRIGHT PLASTIC WITH DELICIOUS, CELLO-WRAPPED POPS AND HARD CANDY!

YOU CAN PLAY THIS DRUM!
Comes complete with two drum sticks. Holds six pops and two pouches of candies. 4⅛" diameter.
49¢

SPOTTED GIRAFFE ON TURNING
Carries two packs of hard candies, six pops. 7½" tall.
39¢

PRICES slightly higher in South and West

BIG STOCKING, 8 TOYS, CANDIES!
Pistol, cowboy, snowman, Santa, soldier, cut-out game, etc. 15 pops. 2 packs of candies. 17½" long.
98¢

REINDEER PULLS SANTA IN WAGON!
15 pops; two pouches of candies. 8" long.
59¢

Made by E. ROSEN CO.

F. W. WOOLWORTH CO.

Warning: You can gain five pounds just by looking at all the sweets pictured in this collection.

bags of candy dangling from the sides. Sears went all out, if not in the amount of candy, at least in the size of the toy, with Santa, a sleigh, and all eight reindeer, a bouquet of lollipops stuck in Santa's backpack.

As time (and we kids) progressed into the 1960s and early 1970s, other types of candy holders supplanted the five-and-ten type. You will likely recall the figures with transparent bodies and the colorful heads of Santa, a snowman, or some other holiday character, filled with colorful hard candy beads. With just a change of the head, the same candy-and-toy combo could become a witch or pumpkin-headed man for Halloween or a colorful rabbit for Easter. You should also remember the giant mesh stockings, often nearly 4 feet tall, stuffed with an assortment of candy and cheap toys. Those were sometimes special added treats along with the toys on Christmas morning, but they more often served as bribes to shut up our whining about "How much longer?" during the weeks before the big day. And then there were those clear plastic trees that looked like barren branches until colorful gumdrops were stuck onto the sharp point of each twig. Just the thought of any of these can be enough to send a nostalgic baby boomer into sugar overload.

Apart from the many kinds of store-bought candy, we also enjoyed an endless variety of Christmas cookies. These could be purchased already baked, as with Archway's sugar cookies shaped like small bells

Candy canes, gumdrop trees, piñatas, giant stockings, Santa-shaped lollipops . . . there seemed to be no end to the variety of yummies available during the Christmas season.

Many of you probably remember your mom making Christmas cookies with clear red plastic cutters just like these, and you might even still be able to recall how they tasted.

and stars frosted with red and green sprinkles, but most of us probably have fond memories of our mothers or grandmothers making their own dough and baking cookies from their own recipes.

Remember the most common Christmas cookie cutters? They were usually made of clear red plastic, and the same designs could be found in stores for decades. They were a bit tricky to use, because of the plethora of details molded into each one: Santa's facial and wardrobe elements, the decorations on the Christmas tree, the reindeer's harness apparatus, and so on. It's no wonder that many people preferred the simpler type of cookie cutter that consisted of only the outline of the figure, leaving it up to the decorator to fill in the blanks.

My mom was never too fired up about spending a lot of time in the kitchen, but at least once during the Christmas season, she would pull herself together and whip up a batch of cookies. I really do not know when or where her recipe originated, but just in case any of you no longer have access to the formula your own mom used, I thought I would present it here. If you choose to try this recipe for yourself, be forewarned that it requires some investment in time and effort—remember, it dates from long before the days of microwave ovens. If you stick with it, however, you'll have a treat that will make your spouse and kids yell for more—only you'll be too tired to hear them. Here goes:

2 cups sifted flour
1 1/4 teaspoons baking powder
1/4 teaspoon salt
1/3 cup Mazola corn oil
3/4 cup sugar
1 teaspoon vanilla
1 egg plus milk to make 1/3 cup

Sift flour, baking powder, and salt into bowl. Add Mazola; blend well with fork or pastry blender (mixture will appear dry). Beat sugar, vanilla, and egg-milk mixture together until light and fluffy. Stir into flour mixture. Chill for 1 hour. Roll out on a floured board or cloth. Cut as desired. Bake in a 400-degree oven for nine minutes. (Baking time may need to be adjusted to prevent burning.)

For variety, who could resist a Whitman's Sampler? You could pick out a piece at random without having the slightest clue as to what type of candy it was, or you could cheat by looking at the chart inside the box lid first.

By themselves, those cookies were tasty enough to make anyone pig out, but they became even more ecstasy-inducing when coated with Mom's recipe for icing:

> Blend 1 1/2 cups Domino confectioner's 10-X powdered sugar into 1 slightly beaten egg white. Add 1 tablespoon melted butter or margarine, 1/8 teaspoon salt and 1/2 teaspoon vanilla extract. Beat until smooth. If icing is thin, add more sugar. Divide icing into several parts and tint as desired with food coloring.

I guess you can tell from these recipes that eating healthy was not a concern of ours. But then again, when it comes to Christmas sweets, it really never has been. That was part of what made the holidays so special: being able to get all the toys you dreamed of and stuff your face with goodies until you're ready to burst. But there were lots of other things to be seen and done as well during those weeks between Thanksgiving and December 25, and the following chapters will examine many of them. Grab a handful of cookies and a chocolate Santa or two, and let's go.

Rudolph and Frosty AND WHAT THEY BEGAT

CHAPTER 2

For decades, if not centuries, Christmas had managed to get along with a basic set of characters who came to embody the holiday. Naturally, there were the figures associated with the biblical accounts of the Nativity, but apart from those, Santa Claus and his eight reindeer had been the only real additions. In the late 1800s, Mrs. Santa Claus and the elves who assisted the jolly old gent made their first appearances in print and art, but they were soon accepted as part of folklore, and that seemed to be the end of it.

Then a new trend began in the years immediately following the Great Depression, although probably no one at the time recognized it as the dawn of a new era in Christmas culture. Department store and mail-order giant Montgomery Ward was on the lookout for a novel giveaway item that could be distributed through its stores for the 1939 holiday season, and the assignment was handed over to advertising copywriter Robert L. May. Several authors have written about the personal turmoil and human drama that May was undergoing while he tried to craft a new Christmas story, inasmuch as his wife was dying and he had the additional burden of caring for their young children. Writing his holiday tale no doubt helped greatly in taking his mind off his real-life troubles.

Knowing that practically any Christmas story had to be about a reindeer, May originally envisioned a deer with a most unusual physical deformity: huge eyes like a cat's, which glowed in the dark. Somehow that seemed more appropriate to a jack-o'-lantern than a Christmas reindeer, so May went back to his typewriter. If the eyes couldn't have

it, perhaps the nose could—so May's deer ended up with a proboscis that shone like a beacon in the night. May decided to call his story *Rollo, the Red-Nosed Reindeer*.

Uh, excuse me—*Rollo*? No one else thought that name sounded right for such a depressed character either. It sounded more like a circus clown, and when May came up with a replacement title, *Reginald, the Red-Nosed Reindeer*, it sounded as if the character should be wearing a monocle and eating fish and chips. Running out of names that started with an *R*, May decided to try Rudolph, and like the little bear's bed in another famous story, somehow this one seemed just right.

Montgomery Ward distributed millions of copies of *Rudolph the Red-Nosed Reindeer* over the next few Christmas seasons, until the paper shortage of World War II put a temporary stop to the custom. May's story was told in rhymed couplets, deliberately aping the structure of *The Night before Christmas*. One innovation that may be attributed to this tale, unless some other diligent researcher manages to prove otherwise, is that it was very likely the first Christmas

When Robert L. May wrote the story of* Rudolph the Red-Nosed Reindeer *as an advertising premium in 1939, he could hardly have known that he was permanently adding a new character to long-established Christmas lore.

As Rudolph's sponsor, Montgomery Ward sold a wide variety of merchandise based on their red-nosed golden boy.

story to anthropomorphize Santa's reindeer, rather than treat them as realistic beasts of burden (or as realistic as they could be, considering that they could fly). With no apparent prior model, May decided to have his reindeer characters live in houses and speak English, both among themselves and to humans such as Santa Claus. This view of the sleigh team shifts back and forth with the earlier, more realistic one in stories to this very day.

When the war was over, in an insanely generous move, Montgomery Ward gave the copyright on the Rudolph character and story to May, allowing him to use it in any manner he wished. He wasted no time in bumping up the merchandising and promotion of Rudolph. One of his first moves was to arrange for a new hardback edition of his story, published by Maxton Books. As Ward's Christmas trademark, a few Rudolph items had been merchandised earlier, but it was when May began handling such matters that his scarlet-nosed gold mine really got into the store aisles in a big way. Out of loyalty to his employer, May saw to it that a few items each year were exclusive to Ward stores, but others could be found far from any areas where Ward was a major retailer.

In 1948, May authorized an animated cartoon version of Rudolph, directed by famed animation pioneer Max Fleischer (of Betty Boop and Popeye fame), who had lost his own studio in 1942 and was now down on his luck, working for a Detroit-based

After Montgomery Ward generously gave Robert May the copyright to his creation, Rudolph merchandising became even bigger and included this puzzle, snow globe, flashlight, and bib (and yes, that is actually a bib I wore as a toddler).

commercial film concern known as Jam Handy Productions. There is some evidence that the cartoon's original release to theaters was sponsored, at least in part, by Montgomery Ward, but the film has been circulating in public-domain prints for so many years that no reference to Ward's remains in the version seen today. Another change is that the version marketed on cheap VHS tapes and DVDs features a theme song spliced onto the beginning and end credits that was not a part of the original 1948 release.

Gene Autry had initially been reluctant to record the Rudolph song by Johnny Marks, but once it became a giant seller for him, he had no qualms about lending his cowboy voice to other Christmas compositions.

That song propelled Rudolph into an even higher stratosphere than where Santa's sleigh habitually traveled. Composer Johnny Marks was married to Robert May's sister, and when he came up with a musical version of Rudolph's red-nose-to-riches saga, the family connection came in handy. It also proved the old adage "Never do business with relatives," as Marks's ownership of the song coupled with May's ownership of the character caused some family friction in the ensuing decades.

Marks shopped his Christmas tune around to every noted singer possible, but they all turned it down for one reason or another. One of his last resorts was crooning cowpoke Gene Autry. Not surprisingly, Autry felt that a song about a talking, red-nosed, flying deer was hardly a fit for a rootin', tootin', two-gun shootin', fancy bootin' cowboy; Autry's wife felt otherwise, however, and used whatever wifely influence she had to persuade her reluctant hubby to give it a try. With little or no confidence in the project, Autry recorded Marks's song in one take at the end of a four-song session and assumed he would never hear anything about it again.

Autry's record of "Rudolph the Red-Nosed Reindeer" was officially released on September 15, 1949, but as few people were buying Christmas records at that time of year, it did not attract much attention until he was talked into performing it live during a rodeo in New York City's Madison Square Garden later that autumn. Autry thought this venue was even more ridiculous for such a production, but he sang it anyway, as an actor in a Rudolph costume—with light-up nose, yet—danced around him. The public stampeded for the music stores, and "Rudolph" became the biggest hit of Autry's career.

The popularity of the song was a considerable boost to May's merchandising efforts, and soon Rudolph was lighting up cash registers in more and more different forms. May even penned a pair of sequels to his original story, neither of which made much of an impression. *Rudolph's Second Christmas* (1951) was never published as a book but did make it onto a narrated record. The plot involves Rudolph trying to help two children whose father runs a broken-down circus with no acts that anyone would want to see. Prefiguring television's much later Island of Misfit Toys, Rudolph discovers a forest of strange animals: a rabbit that creeps like a turtle, a turtle that runs like a rabbit, a barking cat and meowing dog, and so forth. Delivering these baffling beasts to the circus saves the day. *Rudolph Shines Again* (1954) did make it

DC Comics published a new issue of the* Rudolph the Red-Nosed Reindeer *comic book each year from 1950 to 1961, and then revived it briefly in the mid-1970s. The comics introduced new characters to the North Pole cast, including Grover Groundhog and villain J. Baddy Bear.

into book form and also was featured on a View-Master reel. Here a clinically depressed Rudolph finds that his nose will not light up as a result of his constant wallowing in self-pity; only when he has to use it to rescue a pair of young bunny rabbits does it glow again, enabling him to return to leading the sleigh through the Christmas skies.

May—like most authors—tried to make lightning strike again by creating other characters. But his stories *Benny the Bunny Liked Beans* (1940) and *Sam, the Scared-est Scarecrow* (1972) failed to make one-ninety-ninth of the impression of his original creation, Rudolph.

More new adventures of Rudolph were related in comic books published annually by National Comics Publications (later known as National Periodical Publications and DC Comics) beginning in 1950. National published a new issue each year until 1961, and then revived the series for a few additional installments in the mid-1970s. Although the comic books carried Robert May's copyright notice, it is uncertain just how much input he had into them; in the early issues, the artwork was handled by Rube Grossman, with the later books crafted by Sheldon Mayer. Grossman also turned out an annual Rudolph newspaper comic strip that told a story in six episodes per week between Thanksgiving and Christmas.

Since it would have been difficult for even the most creative writer to come up with story after story using only Rudolph, Santa, and the eight traditional reindeer—Dasher through Blitzen—several new characters were introduced who would recur in other Rudolph merchandise in the future. Chief among these was Grover Groundhog, a trouble-prone pest who gave Rudolph a sawed-off sidekick with whom to banter. Also in the mix were Winky and Blinky, twin elves who constantly argued and fought with each other. And since the North Pole would have been pretty dull without a villain, J. Baddy Bear perennially tried to steal toys or otherwise rain on Rudolph's parade.

In the 1951 story, Rudolph and Grover corner Baddy in his cave, where the plucky groundhog attacks the giant bear, only to receive a swat from a hairy paw.

RUDOLPH: Hey, you can't hit Grover! If you hit HIM, you have to hit ME, too!

BADDY: Really?

(SPLAT!)

RUDOLPH (in a heap on the floor): Obliging sort of chap, isn't he?

Other issues added details about Rudolph's nose that were not previously evident. At various times it was revealed that the olfactory organ produced not only light, but also heat, as when he had to use it to melt the snow that Baddy Bear had caused to pile up in front of Santa's workshop door. Even more remarkably, it turned out that it could generate electricity. When Rudolph and Grover were stranded far from the workshop and needed to send a message in Morse code, Rudolph discovered that by concentrating very hard, he could cause his nose to blink the proper sequence of flashes.

Some of the comic book characters were incorporated into other merchandise, most notably a series of Rudolph reels issued by View-Master beginning in the early 1950s. Anyone who grew up during those years will remember the beautifully crafted settings and figures that were common to all View-Master productions. Originally, *Rudolph the Red-Nosed Reindeer* was issued as a single reel, retelling May's original story in seven frames. In the mid-1950s, View-Master began packaging its reels in sets of three and took the occasion to produce a 3-D version of May's 1954 sequel, *Rudolph Shines Again*. To fill the other two reels in that packet, View-Master reached into the comic books and newspaper comics and pulled out a pair of stories that, if they had not appeared in print before, were almost certainly inspired by National Comics' publications.

View-Master produced beautifully crafted scenes from the original Rudolph story, as well as a few of its sequels.

One reel tells the story of how Baddy Bear is caught stealing candy canes from Santa's storage room and, as revenge, determines to make Rudolph's nose obsolete for good. He sets to work with miles of neon tubing and fashions for himself a battery-operated space suit, complete with neon halo over his head. The gullible Santa is more than willing to give Baddy's new glow a try, but Rudolph has to come to the rescue once again when the bruin's battery does not keep going . . . and going . . . and going.

The third reel introduces Rudolph's cranky Uncle Bigby, the Blue-Nosed Reindeer. Uncle Bigby was an import from the Rudolph newspaper strip, where he was the starring character in the 1953 series. Seemingly modeled on a combination of Ebenezer Scrooge and Uncle Scrooge McDuck—with the worst qualities of both—Uncle Bigby lives up to his "blue-nosed" reputation by telling Santa that such things as Christmas and toys are frivolous and nonsensical. Storming off in high dudgeon, the old crab finds himself trapped on an ice floe in the Arctic waters, kept unwelcome company by a polar bear. Arriving in Santa's sleigh, Rudolph discovers a new use for his nose by aiming its rays through a magnifying glass, giving the polar bear third-degree burns on his derriére and saving Uncle Bigby. As we might have expected all along, the former miser changes his ways and donates stacks of money to help Santa's cause, with his blue nose changing to the same shade of red as his famous nephew's.

Eventually the *Rudolph Shines Again* reel was discontinued, and the Baddy and Uncle Bigby stories were combined with the original to create the Rudolph packet that View-Master sold for many more years. The illustrated booklet that accompanied this set of reels proved once again the seeming inconsistency in the treatment of the reindeer. Although they are obviously sentient and can converse with Santa, one illustration shows the nine deer—led by Rudolph—pulling the sleigh through the sky, with Santa wielding a whip to make them go faster. It seems Santa wasn't out to win any awards from the Humane Society.

Since May had licensed Rudolph to Maxton Publishing, that company's version of the original story had been the only one available in book form. That changed in 1958, when Little Golden Books first issued its *Rudolph the Red-Nosed Reindeer* title. It was illustrated by children's book stalwart Richard Scarry, who applied his distinctive style to adapt some of the illustrations that had accompanied the story going all the way back to its Montgomery Ward days. The text was no longer May's original rhyming couplets, but a new prose rendition credited to Barbara Shook Hazen. One of Hazen's newly added scenes created a couple of pages that were later revised.

Embarrassed by the others' taunts about his nose, in the original 1958 version

Rudolph's miserly Uncle Bigby, the Blue-Nosed Reindeer, was introduced in a 1953 newspaper strip and later appeared in 3-D form in one of the View-Master reels. The old grouch combined all the worst traits of Ebenezer Scrooge and Uncle Scrooge McDuck.

Rudolph hides inside a toy pirate chest. One page depicts him climbing into the chest, and another shows him peering out from under the lid as the other reindeer help make toys (how they are able to handle workshop tools with hooves instead of fingers is not made clear). For undisclosed reasons, in 1976 these two pages were changed to show Rudolph hiding behind a holly bush, where his nose blends in with the red berries. An educated guess might be that Golden Books received complaints from parents about encouraging children to climb inside heavy containers and close the lid after them; whatever the case, for those two pages, an unidentified illustrator had to try to re-create Richard Scarry's style in order to match the preceding and following images. Most kids probably did not notice, but the difference in color styling and character design is definitely glaring.

Without a doubt, the second-biggest boost to Rudolph's worldwide fame—after the 1949 hit song—was the 1964 television debut of the stop-motion animated *Rudolph the Red-Nosed Reindeer* special produced by Videocraft International (later known as

Above: ***Eventually Little Golden Books' edition of the Rudolph tale, illustrated by Richard Scarry, managed to eclipse even the original one by Robert May.*** **Right:** ***When the Rankin/Bass animated version of the Rudolph story premiered on NBC-TV in 1964, narrated by Burl Ives, the red-nosed reindeer "went down in history" even more than he had in his earlier incarnations.***

Rankin/Bass Productions). The story of this production is a tale all its own and beyond the scope of this book. I should point out, however, that screenplay writer Romeo Muller basically discarded all previous versions of the story, including the May–Montgomery Ward original and any of the comic

HERMEY

YUKON CORNELIUS

SAM THE SNOWMAN

ELF

SANTA

GE

General Electric

PRESENTS ANOTHER FULL COLOR

Fantasy Hour

"THE STORY OF RUDOLPH THE RED-NOSED REINDEER"

Again this year!

BURL IVES TELLS THE STORY!

Burl Ives, world famous folk singer and story teller narrates and sings throughout this journey into the wonderful world of fantasy.

ORIGINAL SCORE AND 7 NEW SONGS BY JOHNNY MARKS, COMPOSER OF THE CLASSIC, "RUDOLPH THE RED-NOSED REINDEER"

Wonderful new songs from the writer who has warmed millions of hearts with his music. Again, it's great entertainment for the whole family from General Electric...the perfect way to start the Holiday season.

"HOLLY JOLLY CHRISTMAS" "SILVER AND GOLD" "THERE'S ALWAYS TOMORROW"

SUNDAY, DECEMBER 5th, ON NBC-TV

3:30 to 4:30 P. M. MST ★ 4:30 to 5:30 P. M. CST

5:30 to 6:30 P. M. EST & PST

book material, in favor of a completely new plot. (Although there is a possible inspiration for the Island of Misfit Toys in May's 1951 *Rudolph's Second Christmas*, it is unlikely that Muller even had access to that unpublished story when working on his script.)

So familiar have Muller's ideas become today that the show is what most people think of when they hear about Rudolph. This has been proven repeatedly in recent years, when most of the non-Rankin/Bass depictions of Rudolph have been allowed to go off the market; even the venerable 1958 Little Golden Book—pirate chest, holly bush, and all—was eventually replaced by a new Golden Book that retold the story from the television show. The Rudolph special also made a big difference in the little deer's appearances (authorized and not) in the larger world of indoor and outdoor decorations.

In the Christmas season following the Gene Autry recording's first wave of popularity in 1949, it seemed that everyone wanted to get into the act. But the next character to emerge from the crowd actually had his origins almost halfway around the year from the Yuletide season.

Steve Nelson and Jack Rollins were two of the many songwriters who felt they could do Rudolph one or more better, but they hardly wanted to wait a whole year. They dashed off a ditty they called "Peter Cottontail," with an eye on the upcoming 1950 Easter season. Although the name Peter Cottontail was not original—Thornton Burgess had used it in a long series of children's stories—the song was the first time it was applied to the bearer of colored eggs and chocolate bunnies. Nelson and Rollins pitched Peter to Gene Autry as a follow-up to his earlier holiday hit, and Autry did not hesitate this time to sing the praises of a cuddly rodent who hippity-hopped down the bunny trail.

With Peter on his way and the 1950 Christmas season looming, Nelson and Rollins introduced Autry to their newest creation: Frosty the Snowman. By now Autry was getting to be an old cowhand at this holiday character stuff, so he knocked out a recording of the chilly new song, and Frosty prepared to take the world by snowstorm.

The song "Frosty the Snowman" was a hit for Christmas 1950, and by the time the holidays rolled around again, the character of Frosty the Snowman was everywhere. The Rudolph merchandise had benefited greatly from its association with the retail king Montgomery Ward, so Frosty hitched his sled to another merchandising monarch, Sears, Roebuck and Company.

The 1951 edition of the Sears Christmas catalog (not yet called a Wish Book) not only featured a Frosty pull toy on the cover, but also splattered the jolly, happy soul all over the interior pages. Sears even had the audacity to compare him to the holiday's previously established salesman: "The most lovable fellow since Santa Claus sets up his exclusive mail order workshop at Sears," the catalog boasted. Seemingly anything and everything that could conceivably have Frosty's image printed on it was featured: clothing of all styles, plus winter accessories such as mittens, scarves, and ear muffs; suspenders; toddler training pants

Hill and Range Songs introduced the character of Frosty the Snowman in 1950, and most of the merchandising followed the lead of this artwork from the original sheet music.

Among the Frosty the Snowman merchandise available for Christmas 1951 was this pull toy and a very similarly designed night-light in the shape of the jolly, happy soul.

(for those junior citizens who leaked instead of melting); a shoulder-strap bag; towels; blankets; figural soap; a music box; lamp; savings bank (for cold cash); squeeze toy; night light; and for those who had had enough of Frosty, a punching bag with his image emblazoned where one's fist should go.

When Frosty's publisher, Hill and Range, set out to make their character the new Rudolph, the company apparently decided to make sure that most of the official merchan-

While most of the Frosty items featured the original design, a few such as this coloring book took a more imaginative approach. Here Frosty looks more like a scarecrow than a snowman.

dise conformed to a standardized image. Thus Frosty's appearance remained consistent throughout it all. (While Rudolph's design could change a bit, everyone knew what a deer was supposed to look like, so he could not stray too far from that.) In traditional snowman style, Frosty's body and head were composed of three round balls, topped with the famous silk hat that brought him to life. A snowflake was embroidered on Frosty's scarf, and matching snowflakes adorned his red mittens. Occasionally yet another snowflake could be seen pinned to his chest, like some sort of badge. Red boots completed his ensemble, although it was left up to the individual artist to decide whether Frosty had legs inside them.

It would take until 1958 for Rudolph to make it into the Little Golden Books series, but Hill and Range got a *Frosty the Snowman* Golden Book on the market for 1951, along with all the other merchandise. The text was credited to Annie North Bedford, a pseudonym used by a number of Golden's staff writers and an inside joke referring to the company's Los Angeles offices on North Bedford Drive. Even more memorable than the text, which frankly did not have much of a plot, were the illustrations by Golden artist Corinne Malvern. She stuck with the established appearance of Frosty but rendered her artwork with such elaborate shading that one could almost believe the paintings were actual photos of a living snowman. Malvern tackled the question of Frosty's feet in an unusual way; while she retained the red boots, she drew no legs connecting said boots with Frosty's lower body, so the boots simply served as moving feet appearing to float eerily in the air.

If Rudolph could have his own comic book series, so could Frosty, and thus, Dell Comics rolled out its first issue of *Frosty the Snowman* in time for Christmas 1951 as well. As with Rudolph's adventures, a new issue was published each year through the early 1960s, but since Frosty was a bit more of a blank slate than Rudolph, his story lines took on more variety. In the very first story of the first comic book, Frosty is asked by some children to judge their

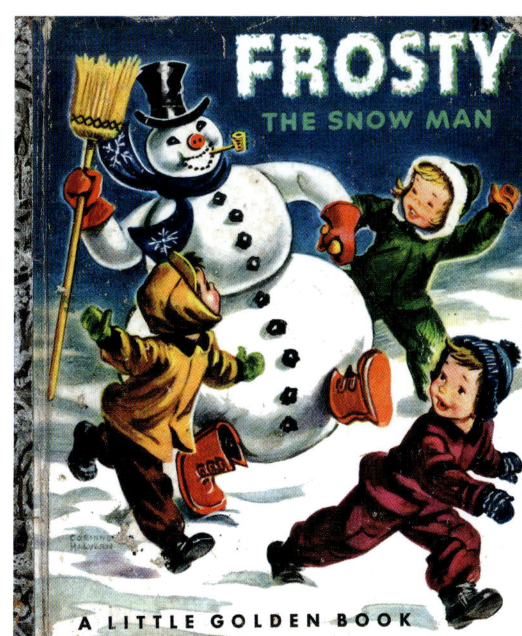

For Little Golden Books'* Frosty the Snowman, *published in 1951, illustrator Corinne Malvern used the Hill and Range artwork as a starting point, but she truly brought the snowy figure to life even more effectively than his magic silk hat.

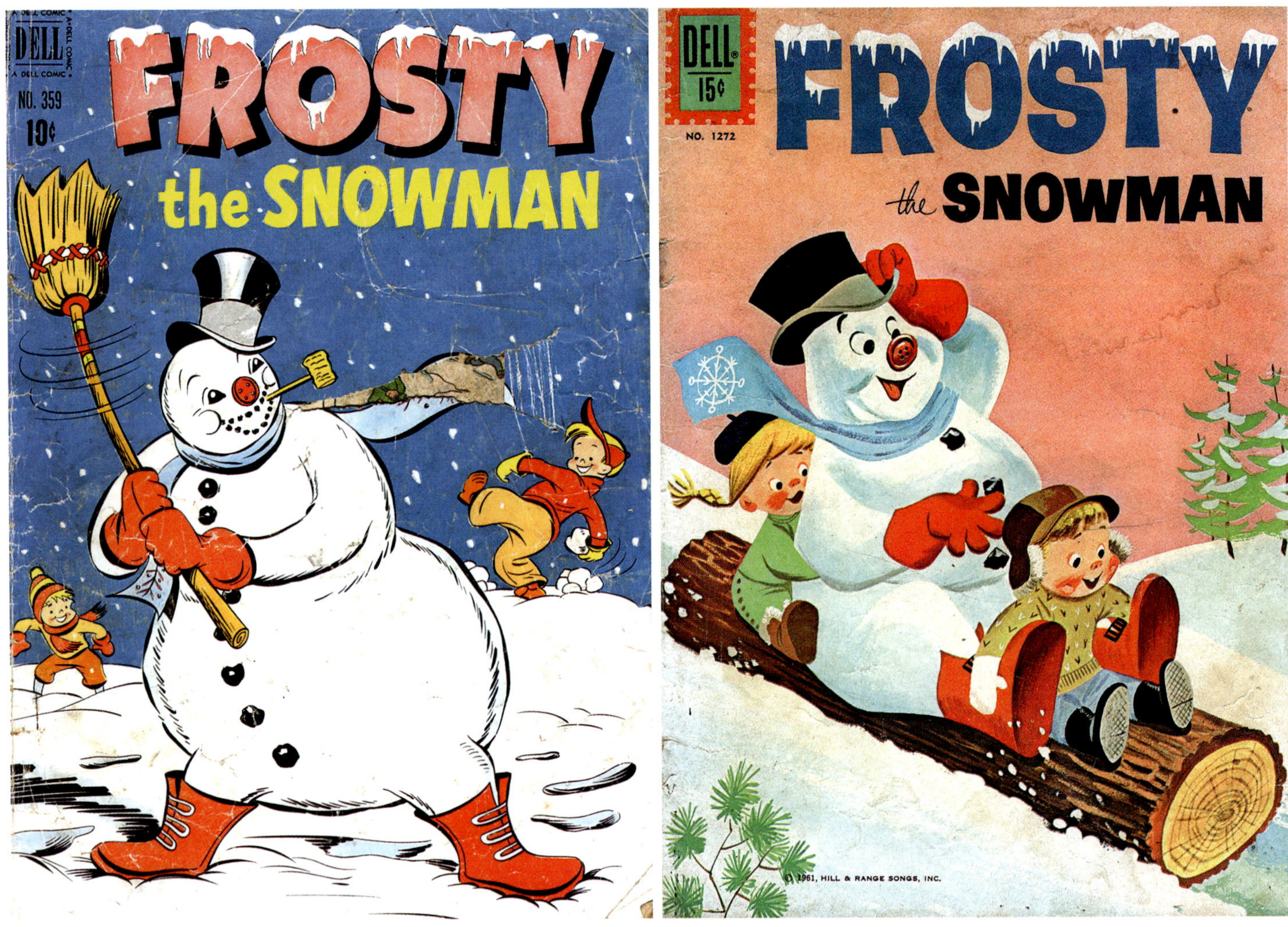

These two issues, separated by a decade, show Dell Comics' evolving concept of Frosty. The one on the left, from 1951, looks much like the Hill and Range/Corinne Malvern interpretation, whereas the one on the right, from 1961, has turned Frosty into a sort of polar W. C. Fields.

snowmen; he does so by placing his magic hat atop each snow dome so everyone can see each sculpture's abilities. Things go horribly awry when one bratty little boy's snowman comes to life, takes the name Freezer, and in true Frankenstein fashion, turns on his own creator. Another story in the same issue has Frosty journeying to the North Pole to help Santa with his Christmas preparations, and future issues continued to move Frosty between the "real world" of children playing in the snow and the more fantastic trappings of Santa's workshop.

During all this initial Frosty fever, the first animated cartoon version of the song made its appearance. It was produced by the popular animation studio United Productions of America (UPA), best known for creating the nearsighted Mister Magoo. UPA's film *Frosty the Snowman* used the same established design of the character, and his few spoken lines apparently were delivered by one of UPA's busiest voice actors, Jerry Hausner.

Another animated version appeared in 1969, when Frosty belatedly received the TV treatment from Rankin/Bass. His half-hour special, narrated by the inimitable Jimmy Durante, became another annual Christmas television classic. Eventually it too supplanted all previous designs of the character, and today when most people think of Frosty, they think of the Rankin/Bass version.

Hill and Range was reaping such a blizzard of money from Frosty's antics that the company decided to try to keep the snowball rolling with other songs that had merchandising potential. Christmas 1951 brought the song "Suzy Snowflake," written by Roy Bennett and Sid Tepper (who later got their groove on and wrote numerous songs for Elvis Presley) and recorded by Rosemary Clooney. The song was successful enough, but since Suzy had even less personality than Frosty, it did not produce much in the way of merchandise.

Hill and Range's attempt for Christmas 1952 was "The Three Little Dwarfs," a creation of Stuart Hamblin, whose quasi-hymn "This Old House" had been a big smash. His Christmas verse introduced the world to Santa's three helpers, improbably named Hardrock, Coco, and Joe. Both Hamblin's song and "Suzy Snowflake" received the animated treatment, but unlike UPA's Frosty short, they were done with stop-motion animation that strongly prefigured the Rankin/Bass style. The *Suzy Snowflake* film even included a cameo appearance by a stop-motion Frosty, helping illustrate the line "If you want to build a snowman, I'll help you make one, one, two, three." Both films received television airplay, which helped popularize their songs, and became legendary for the many years they were run on WGN-TV in Chicago. The sheer nostalgia and tradition of viewing the films each Christmas have given them a status that the writers of the underlying musical compositions could only dream about.

All of these additional Christmas characters came about through the medium of popular music, but there was another cate-

This chocolate Frosty from 1989 was one of the first pieces of merchandise to employ the 1969 Rankin/Bass design of the character. As with Rudolph, eventually the Rankin/Bass version came to overshadow all the others. You have to love the idea of pure Belgian milk chocolate made in Canada.

gory of holiday personalities that, like Rudolph, originated in the retail world. One of them actually predated Rudolph but never attained anywhere near the red-nosed animal's fame. In 1937, radio producer Lindsay MacHarrie conceived the idea of a children's serial that would be broadcast in daily fifteen-minute installments between Thanksgiving and Christmas, giving ample opportunity for companies that relied heavily on Christmas sales—mainly department stores, with their toy departments—to sponsor the series in each city where it ran. MacHarrie enlisted the writing services of Glanville "Glan" Heisch for his creation, which turned out to be the much-beloved series *The Cinnamon Bear.*

The plot seemed to be heavily derived from the successful series of Oz books—in particular, the ones that were then being written by Ruth Plumly Thompson, who had succeeded Oz creator L. Frank Baum after his death. The titular bear, Paddy O'Cinnamon, conducts two children, Judy and Jimmy Barton, through his home country of Maybeland in search of the antique silver star that belongs atop the youngsters' Christmas tree. The object, which obviously has more sentimental than monetary value, has been stolen by the duplicitous Crazy Quilt Dragon, who has an obsessive love for shiny things. As one might expect, it takes all twenty-six episodes before the star is safely placed on the tree and the characters are able to wish everyone a Merry Christmas.

The Cinnamon Bear boasted production standards unusually high for its type of programming. Several episodes featured original songs, and the cast was made up of a staggering number of present and future character actors, including Joseph Kearns, later Mr. Wilson on *Dennis the Menace*, as the dragon; Gale Gordon, Lucille Ball's slow-burn partner in comedy; Howard McNear, Floyd the Barber on *The Andy Griffith Show*; and Frank Nelson of *Jack Benny Show* fame. Paddy O'Cinnamon was played by Bud Duncan, with an accent that suggested shamrocks bloomin' every time he opened his mouth, begorrah. A few years later, Duncan would trade in his Irish accent for a hillbilly one and portray comic strip redneck Snuffy Smith in a pair of live-action movies for the Monogram studio.

The Cinnamon Bear became a Christmas season tradition in many large cities but was particularly popular in the Midwest and on the West Coast. Whatever local department store signed on as sponsor had the

SANTA CLAUS SAYS:

The fluffy Cinnamon Bear asked me to give you these songs. SOoo, every afternoon ('cept Saturday and Sunday) when mommie tunes in the "Cinnamon Bear" over KFBK . . you can hum with the Bear when HE sings. That's 4:45 o'clock. P. S. – Please come to see me often . . and all my shiny toys . . in

WEINSTOCK-LUBIN'S
AUDITORIUM, MEZZANINE

Weinstock-Lubin, the department store sponsor for the Cinnamon Bear radio broadcasts in Sacramento, gave away these folios of sheet music for the show's original songs.

option of offering several different tie-in items to remind the kids to listen: Wieboldt's in Chicago gave away replica silver stars with Paddy O'Cinnamon's grinning face plastered in the center; Weinstock-Lubin's in Sacramento offered booklets with the sheet music for the series' songs; Lipman's in Portland, Oregon, had a costumed Cinnamon Bear with whom kids could have their photos taken in addition to—and, sometimes instead of—Santa Claus. The serial continued to run on local radio stations for decades, even after the television era arrived, and became a much-anticipated harbinger of the Christmas season to millions.

Anything that successful usually breeds imitators, and so it was with *The Cinnamon Bear* in Radioland. The next Christmas season, another radio syndication company offered a rival serial, *Jonathan Thomas and His Christmas on the Moon*. But unlike its predecessor, with its all-star cast, this serial featured no familiar voices. The title role was not even played by a real child, but obviously by one of the many women who provided "little kid" voices for radio shows and animated cartoons of the period.

The plot was, if anything, even more loosely structured than that of the Oz-inspired *Cinnamon Bear*. Talkative tot Jonathan Thomas, whose name may have been meant to evoke memories of Christopher Robin, finds his teddy bear, Guz, purloined by two elves who slide down a moonbeam and make off with the stuffed animal. In rapid succession, Jonathan follows them to the moon, meets the more-than-a-little-pixilated Man in the Moon, and learns that Santa Claus has been kidnapped by the evil Squeebobblems (I'm not making this up). For twenty-six episodes, Jonathan and the rhyme-spouting Man in the Moon wander throughout the magical countries of the moon, meeting friend and foe alike, before the inevitable happy ending and Santa's rescue.

Radio historian Harlan Zinck has pointed out that the main contribution of the Jonathan Thomas serial to the Christmas retail scene came about because of being number two. In most cities where *The Cinnamon Bear* had aired the year before, its sponsorship had been picked up by one of the larger stores—and those sponsors tended to continue having the show aired each Christmas season. *Jonathan Thomas and His Christmas on the Moon* provided an outlet for smaller stores to have their own radio outlet for plugging their wares during the holiday season, especially when broadcast on another station opposite Paddy O'Cinnamon and friends.

Regardless of its value to sales during the 1938 Christmas season, the Jonathan Thomas story proved not to have the same sticking power as *The Cinnamon Bear*. Part of this was due to its plodding pace, where sometimes it seemed to take several episodes for the characters to accomplish anything. Many of those characters had ill-developed or one-note personalities to begin with, among them Gorgonzola the Horse (whose voice is a Jimmy Durante imitation), Whiskery Bill the cranky squirrel, Sir Algy the Walrus (who claims to be the same one who shared literary space with a carpenter in *Through the Looking Glass*), and others who move in and out of the story inconsequentially.

In 1940, a New York-based syndication company came up with a series known as *Jump Jump of Holiday House*. Despite what the title might indicate, the show was distributed year-round. The title character is an elf with a sped-up voice (predating the more famous singing chipmunks by almost twenty years) who visits his friend, the lovely Mary Holiday, to be told a different fairy tale each weekday. All of the voices were provided by a cast of two; scores of children undoubtedly fell in love with Mary McConnell's sweet voice as Mary Holiday, while busy radio actor Harry Hickox played everyone else.

In the years after World War II, the show was revamped into what the producers hoped would be a merchandising bonanza, and to tie in with that campaign, a new twenty-five-episode serial, *Jump Jump and the Ice Queen*, was produced. It followed the pattern established by *The Cinnamon Bear*, which was still running annually in many markets, and the long-forgotten Jonathan Thomas serial. The plot is established in the first episode, when orphanage

The squeaky-voiced elf Jump Jump was introduced to the children's radio market in 1940, but he was not originally conceived as strictly a Christmas character.
FIRST GENERATION RADIO ARCHIVES

resident Tim decides to pay a personal visit to Santa Claus to find out whether the jolly old gent plans to visit the orphanage this year. The chattering Jump Jump leads him to Holiday House, where Mary Holiday and her friends await. In short order, they all learn that Santa's reindeer have been abducted by the dreaded Ice Queen, crippling his chances to make his annual journey. Tim, Jump Jump, Mary, and their motley crew set out to save the day.

Although child actor Johnny McGovern was brought in to play the central role of Tim, the rest of the male voices came from the versatile larynx of Harry Hickox, who gave distinctive personalities to such eccentrics as Sleepy Slim the lion (it is impossible to listen to his dialogue without beginning to yawn) and the irrepressible clown Achi Paggli (who explains that his name is Pagliacci turned sideways, a joke no doubt lost on the juvenile audience), as well as Santa Claus himself. Mary McConnell continued her original role of Mary Holiday and also switched gears completely to play the evil Ice Queen.

The group confronts the villain in her lair, where the icy-hearted queen commits the cardinal sin of insulting the precious Mary Holiday, referring to her as a "silly woman" because she wears an apron and tells fairy tales. (This scene takes on added psychological depth when one realizes that McConnell is talking to herself in it.) As if one could not guess, the Ice Queen is defeated, and Santa sets out on his gift-giving journey, armed with a supply of toys made in the images of Jump Jump and his friends—a none-too-subtle plug for the new line of merchandise that was being offered for the 1948 Christmas season.

It might be worth noting that the final episode has a different spin on things than the two major Christmas radio serials that preceded it. Jonathan Thomas makes it very clear that the whole adventure had been a dream, explaining its resemblance to the Lewis Carroll stories. *The Cinnamon Bear* leaves the question of its reality more open to conjecture, as Judy and Jimmy do wake up in the middle of the action but later hear Paddy O'Cinnamon's voice coming from the toy bear on their Christmas tree. *Jump Jump and the Ice Queen* throws the "it was all a dream" concept right out the frosted windowpane, however, as Christmas Day at the orphanage brings a visit from not only Santa, but also Jump Jump, Mary, Achi Paggli, Sleepy Slim, and the whole cast for all the residents to see in person.

By the time Jump Jump's Christmas adventure was produced, television was making rapid inroads into radio's previously undisputed territory, and with the added appeal of the visual medium, department stores in the larger cities began to develop

In 1948, actors Harry Hickox and Mary McConnell recorded a new series of Jump Jump radio shows in which the plucky elf had to help rescue Santa Claus from the evil clutches of the Ice Queen.
FIRST GENERATION RADIO ARCHIVES

more and more Christmas characters of their own to help out during the joyous selling—er, holiday—season. In 1946, the giant Marshall Field's store in Chicago decided to take its annual Christmas display windows in a new direction by highlighting the completely original figure of Uncle Mistletoe.

The story of how Marshall Field's assigned its creative personnel to come up with a Christmas character makes it sound as if they might have been looking jealously at what Chicago rival Montgomery Ward had done with Rudolph. Artist Johanna Osborne designed a Dickens-vintage little man dressed in a long, red frock coat and black top hat, with gauzy wings to help him flitter about from place to place. Originally the store was going to call him Uncle Marshall, but perhaps fearing that might be taking commercialism a little too far, they finally settled on the name Uncle Mistletoe. He made his debut in Field's 1946 windows and soon became an annual icon for the children of Chicago.

As the Uncle Mistletoe legend grew, his position as Santa's assistant and office manager was established. Besides his annual appearance in Field's window displays and other advertising, the jolly uncle and his white-haired wife, Aunt Holly, had their own display area on the store's eighth floor. Uncle Mistletoe's domicile was known as Cozy Cloud Cottage, where children met not only a live Uncle Mistletoe and Aunt Holly, but jolly old St. Nick too.

Uncle Mistletoe, in puppet form, became the star of his own holiday-season television show in Chicago in 1948. Reportedly, it was such a big hit that it continued until the following June. It must have been a bit strange to see a Christmas character cavorting across the TV screen in late spring, but this is what Chicago broadcasting historians claim. The show subsequently returned each Christmas season through the early 1950s, adding more characters to the core cast, including Tony Pony, a living rocking horse; Humphrey Mouse; Michael O'Hare, a rabbit with an Irish accent; and Obadiah Pig.

All of these characters appeared in an Uncle Mistletoe record released by Simon and Schuster as part of the Big Golden Records line. The record's release was accompanied by a Little Golden Book featuring Uncle Mistletoe, which told a very different story but was obviously meant to help spread the cheerful little elf's goodwill to all men, whether or not they lived within Marshall Field's marketing area. Both the record and the book contain references that, though probably unintentional, seem strange coming from a property owned by such a prominent department store. In the record, as Uncle Mistletoe and the others help Santa prepare for his Christmas Eve flight, there is a reference to Michael O'Hare polishing Rudolph's nose. The book contains the following sentences on its next-to-last page: "Aunt Holly made certain they were warmly buttoned up. Then Uncle Mistletoe led the way to the busy Sleighport and the high-piled sleigh. Santa took the reins from Cinnamon Bear. He whistled to the team, and away they all flew." Considering that Rudolph and the Cinnamon Bear had been so long associated with Field's competitors Montgomery Ward and Weiboldt's, their appearances in the Uncle

Uncle Mistletoe was Santa's Dickens-inspired business manager, Marshall Field's 1946 contribution to the growing Christmas cast of characters.

Rival Chicago department store icons Uncle Mistletoe (Marshall Field's) and the Cinnamon Bear (Wieboldt's) put aside their differences and work for a common Claus in the Uncle Mistletoe Little Golden Book.

Mistletoe adventures seem to have slipped past someone in the store's review process.

While Uncle Mistletoe was making merry in Chicago, Emile Alline, a representative from New Orleans's Maison Blanche department store, visited the Windy City and saw what was happening with Field's Mr. Pickwick look-alike. Alline went back to his southern clime with the idea of doing something similar at his store, but his resulting creation did not resemble Uncle Mistletoe in the least—except for the fact that both of them had wings.

Alline's Maison Blanche Christmas mascot, Mr. Bingle, debuted in 1948. (You will notice that the store and the character shared the same initials.) Rather than being a Victorian gentleman, Bingle was a snowman with an upside-down ice cream cone for a hat. He was generally seen carrying a candy cane, and his wings were made from holly leaves. Like his Chicago predecessor, Bingle was used heavily in store decorations and promotions, and also appeared in marionette form. Maison Blanche hired puppeteer Edwin "Oscar" Isentrout to perform Bingle shows in the display windows, and later in the store itself, and when television came to New Orleans, Bingle moved into that medium as well.

Maison Blanche was owned by a New York-based department store chain known as City Stores, and when the parent company saw how Bingle could make cash registers jingle, it decided to try him out in other markets. In Birmingham, Alabama, where City Stores owned Loveman's department store, it built the promotions for Christmases 1950, 1951, and 1952 around the little snowman. Bingle was featured in window displays and exterior decorations, just as in New Orleans, as well as a daily television program broadcast from the store. In Memphis, Bingle made annual appearances at the City Stores outlet Lowenstein's throughout the 1960s. In his Memphis TV incarnation, Bingle was paired with an attractive young lady known as Miss Holly, with whom he bantered about Lowenstein's merchandise that was perfect for gift giving.

Cleveland, Ohio, brought a latecomer into the holiday scene when the Halle Brothers department store introduced Mr. Jingeling in 1956. As his backstory explained, Jingeling was a locksmith who had ended

This cheerful snowman with holly wings and an upside-down ice cream cone for a hat is Mr. Bingle, introduced by the Maison Blanche department store of New Orleans in 1948.

Above left: ***Mr. Bingle became a beloved Christmas personality for kids in Louisiana and eventually in the other cities where stores called on Bingle's services during the holiday season.*** DONNIE PITCHFORD **Above right:** ***In the early 1950s, Bingle appeared at Loveman's in Birmingham, Alabama, in the form of a giant decoration, as a puppet show on television, and in the animated window displays.***

up as the "keeper of the keys to Toyland." Naturally, that fit in well with his appearances in Halle's toy department and was continued in his yearly television appearances. His costume was a green elflike suit, but his most distinguishing physical feature was his bald head with two tufts of hair sticking up like wings above his ears.

Several different Cleveland actors played Mr. Jingeling through the years, but the one who became most associated with the character was Earl Keyes, who stayed with it for

It is not known just who attempted to make a new Christmas star out of this character, known as Chris Jingle. Judging from the illustration here, it seems that he was originally presented as a stuffed toy with a vinyl head.

thirty years. Jingeling's television career ended in the late 1960s, when Halle's was bought out by Marshall Field's. It is not known whether Field's attempted to unseat Mr. Jingeling in favor of Uncle Mistletoe, but the end result was that Jingeling remained a fixture in the various branch stores in the Cleveland area. Earl Keyes made his last public appearance as Jingeling in 1995, after which he slowly succumbed to Alzheimer's disease, but other performers continue the role even today in personal appearances, if not on television.

With Mr. Jingeling, Uncle Mistletoe, and Mr. Bingle holding down their respective parts of the country, department stores everywhere else began to come up with their own characters. More often than not, the main area of these personalities' influence was in the endless variety of Santa-themed TV shows on local stations across the nation. In 1948, the J. L. Hudson store of Detroit sponsored a show featuring Santa and his helper Jump Jump, who apparently had no connection with the radio character of the same name. Detroit's video version of Jump Jump was one of the first acting jobs for Dick Beals, who later won fame as the voice of Speedy Alka-Seltzer and played many other cartoon voice roles. In San Francisco, the White House department store (interestingly, Maison Blanche is French for White House) had Happy Holly, who appeared on television in the 1950s to introduce the local Christmas show. A now-unidentified store in Wichita, Kansas, teamed Santa with a partner named Toyboy, which sounds more like the name of a comic book villain of some sort. In Salinas, California, Santa had the more dependable help of Mrs. Santa, played by Judy Oates, on his daily show.

A toy store in Winston-Salem, North Carolina, brought that city Marco Polar Bear, another in Santa's endless arsenal of helpers. This one was armed with a toy-making machine that spit out the latest doodad the sponsor wanted to push. In Rapid City, South Dakota, Kmart sponsored the Jolly Postman, played by John Clement, who opened kids' mail to Santa Claus and read it over the air, no doubt in violation of many postal regulations and the Privacy Act. The TV Santa in Buffalo, New York, had not one but three new characters helping him with his broadcasting chores: Freezy the Polar Bear and elves Forgetful and Grumbles (what, no Hardrock, Coco, and Joe?).

Prior to Mr. Jingeling's advent in Cleveland, two different stations and two different sponsors had been responsible for Santa shows. Both versions starred John Saunders in the title role but otherwise took vastly different approaches. In 1951, *Variety* noted: "A veteran at the Santa Claus programming technique, Saunders this year has added a make-believe voice of Twinkletoes, one of his North Pole playmates. There is no direct commercial spiel at any point in the show, and only Coca-Cola notices come with clever jack-in-the-box windup." This is the

Local television stations across the country produced their own Santa Claus shows during the holidays. WBEN-TV in Buffalo, New York, introduced viewers to two of Santa's many elfin helpers, Forgetful and Grumbles.

only known instance of Coca-Cola bringing its long-running Santa print ad campaign to the local kids' TV market, although there could be other examples yet undocumented.

Saunders was forging ahead bravely when *Variety* caught up with him again in 1954, but the show biz journal was decidedly less impressed with his new sponsor, the S. S. Kresge chain of variety stores (the company that later became Kmart). The reviewer wrote: "If you ever wondered how commercial you can make Santa, take a squint at the 13-minute cross-the-board Kresge stanza. Here's toyland with a huge Kresge sign in the background, and right behind Santa. Kids are invited to write in with the best writers picked to appear. Winners are given gifts—and nice ones at that—but as the gift is handed to the moppet, a dollar-and-cent super virtually blots out the gift but no doubt impresses the youngster at home that shopping values are best at Kresge. Oh yes, if he wants to write a letter, he has to get his entry blank at any one of the Kresge stores." Assisting Santa in his mercenary duties, as dictated by Kresge, were Pat Oliver as Jingles and the ever-unseen Twinkletoes, here identified as "Saunders' voice on a sped-up disk" (making Twinkletoes sound an awful lot like Jump Jump, we assume).

Another character who was similar to these others but apparently existed to serve a more noble purpose was Kewtee Bear. His origins are somewhat mysterious after all these years, but evidence seems to indicate that his franchise was launched for the Christmas season of either 1955 or 1956. Kewtee was co-created by radio actor Alan Reed, who, half a decade later, eclipsed all of his previous roles when he became the unmistakable voice of Fred Flintstone. Reed's assistants in the "Kewtee kaper" were Bert Stout and Truman Quigley, and together they created a unified marketing plan for their fuzzy friend. Kewtee dolls were manufactured by the famed Knickerbocker toy company, Alan Reed put his acting skills to work narrating a record featuring the bear for the Columbia label, and Wonder Books told the little bruin's origin story in *Kewtee Bear: Santa's Helper*.

Kewtee Bear was the mascot of clubs formed to encourage kids to help those less fortunate than themselves. Like the mysterious Chris Jingle, Kewtee appears to have originated as a stuffed animal with a plastic face.

With the Knickerbocker connection, it seems obvious that Kewtee was meant to be associated with a particular store—toy or department or, to be ideal, department store toy department—in each city where he appeared. His reason for existing, though, went a bit deeper than mere sales. At the end of Kewtee's Wonder Book, Santa Claus explains that he wants the pink-nosed plantigrade to start a series of Santa's Helpers Clubs. "Through these clubs you will make helpers out of every child in every city and town," old St. Nick says. "The children must bring in toys—old or new, used or unused. Then they can be given to other boys and girls to make them happy." The book concludes, "As Christmas comes around each year, Kewtee Bear can be seen passing out badges to new members of Santa's Helpers Clubs, and he helps the children share their toys."

In the book, Kewtee was pictured much as the Knickerbocker dolls must have looked, with a vinyl face attached to a fluffy plush body. Considering that the Kewtee Bear program seems to have run its course over only a couple of seasons, it is no wonder the character is remembered mainly for the pieces of tie-in merchandise he produced.

No matter how commercial the various Christmas characters were, be they international celebrities such as Rudolph and Frosty, hometown heroes such as Uncle Mistletoe and Mr. Jingeling, or philanthropic like Kewtee Bear, they all did their part to make Christmas a little more special. And if they helped push more merchandise through the department stores' automatic doors while doing so—well, isn't that what Christmas is all about?

Stories TO FALL ASLEEP ON CHRISTMAS EVE BY

CHAPTER 3

When you were a youngster—no matter how long ago that may have been—didn't it seem that Christmas would never get here? The catalogs or Wish Books would arrive shortly after Labor Day, and then came the long haul through September, October, November, and the first three weeks of December before the big day finally arrived. (Of course, we all know the year is shorter nowadays, and Christmas gets here a week or two after the Fourth of July, right?)

So how could antsy kids manage to occupy the endless days while waiting for Christmas? One way was through enjoying Christmas-themed books. The vast majority of mass-marketed Christmas storybooks were published by Little Golden Books and Wonder Books, with the various series by Whitman running close behind. Between all of these various companies could be found a Christmas book of any type.

One of the surest ways of getting a kid's mind off calendar watching was to get him or her involved in some sort of craft activity. *Things to Make and Do for Christmas*, published by Wonder Books subsidiary Treasure Books in 1953, gave a string of such projects to occupy young hands and minds. It can be difficult to find intact copies of the book after more than fifty years, simply because so many of the projects required the mutilation of the book itself. Hosted by two more in the endless string of Santa's elves, Mr. Snip and Mr. Tape, the book gives detailed instructions on how to make a figure of Santa out of an inflated red balloon with a face and appendages attached; simple Christmas cards and envelopes; a collage-type *Night before Christmas* scene; paper chains; and a Nativity scene with stand-up figures.

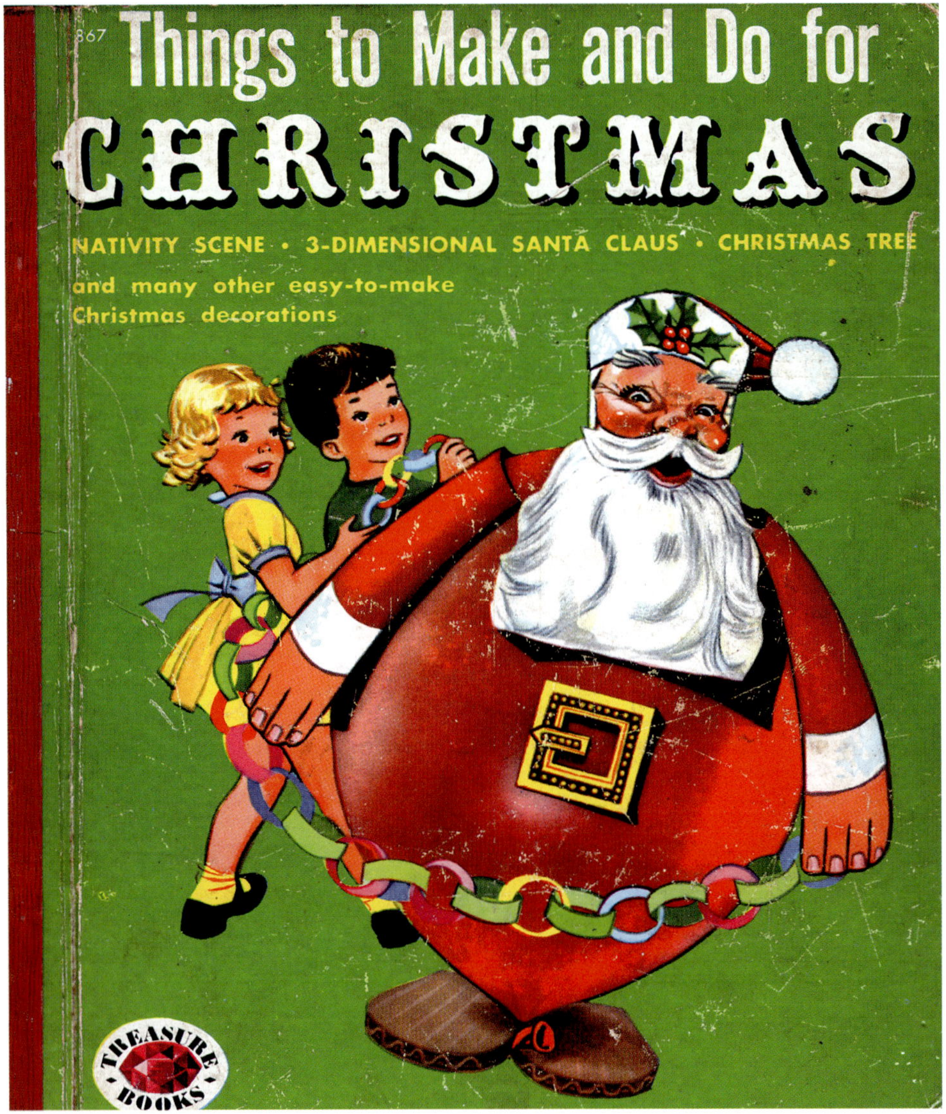

The Wonder Book of Christmas (1951) took a similarly scattershot approach but, instead of offering time-consuming crafts, featured Christmas selections from literature and music. As might be expected, *'Twas the Night before Christmas* is presented in its unabridged text, but some of the others suffer from space limitations. Dickens's *A Christmas Carol* was reduced to 123 words, concentrating only on the Cratchit family's dinner and with Scrooge nowhere in sight. The Christmas story from the Bible fared little better, limited to ten

typeset lines but at least retaining the most important points. Other short poems and stories filled the remainder of the pages, no doubt giving something to use as bedtime material during the weeks leading up to Christmas.

Books such as these usually balanced the sacred and secular aspects of the Christmas holidays, but occasionally one went totally toward the former. *The Story of the Christ Child*, also published by Wonder Books (1953), goes in almost the opposite extreme from the abbreviated Nativity story in *The Wonder Book of Christmas*. In order to make Luke's and Matthew's accounts of the birth of Jesus occupy the required number of pages, much padding had to be done. This was obvious from the paragraph that began the first page: "A long time ago, in a town called Nazareth, there lived a beautiful maiden named Mary. Mary was very happy. She loved her garden and spent many sunny days caring for her flowers and feeding the birds and little animals that scampered in the garden." Only three sentences, and already we have been told more about Mary than can be found in the entire Bible.

Another genre of stories used the background or events of the first Christmas as the launching point for a wholly fictional tale. In 1947, Charles Tazewell, who had already provided readers with a little taste of heaven in *The Littlest Angel* (1939), wrote *The Small One*, relating how an unwanted donkey, weakened by age and work, is chosen to carry Mary and her precious cargo to Bethlehem. The story gained much popularity from being narrated on radio by Bing Crosby each year, and much later, in the 1970s, it became the basis for an animated featurette from the Walt Disney Studios. Of much the same flavor was *Why the Chimes Rang*, a 1906 tale by Raymond MacDonald Alden. In it, the most lavish Christmas Eve offerings of the well-heeled populace fail to cause the cathedral's chimes to ring out in approval, until the highly anticipated sound is released by a poor boy's donation of his last coin. This story also became a radio perennial, told year after year by Harold Peary in his characterization of the Great Gildersleeve.

Charles Tazewell followed up his earlier hits* The Littlest Angel *(1939) and* The Small One *(1947) with another diminutive hero,* The Littlest Snowman *(1955).

Charles Tazewell obviously had an affinity for characters with variations of "small" or "little" in their names, because in 1955 he followed up his earlier hits with *The Littlest Snowman*. Unlike the others, this character appeared in more than one plot over the next few years, but each one seemed to have the same concept. Proving his selflessness, the Littlest Snowman would annually sacrifice his own life to save his fellow townspeople from some calamity or another, only to be rebuilt and brought back at the end of each tale. In one, he melts while fighting the fire from the blazing town Christmas tree. In another with an even more bizarre concept, he saves the day when it appears the town is not going to have a white Christmas. How, you ask with your eyes bulging? The snowman eats ice cream and snow cones until he is overweight, then climbs to the top of the Christmas tree and allows the north wind to blow him to pieces, scattering multiflavored snowflakes throughout the town. No one ever said the life of a snowman was easy.

Perhaps the most perfect evocation of the Christmas season for those baby boomers who grew up in the 1950s and 1960s is Wonder Books' *Waiting for Santa Claus* (1952). The plot (such as it is) follows a typical postwar suburban family as they decorate their house, make Christmas cookies, visit a downtown department store to see Santa, buy outdoor lights, pick out a live tree, read *'Twas the Night before Christmas* before going to bed, open presents, go to church, receive a visit from Grandma and Grandpa—oh, you can probably fill in the blanks from your own memory, can't you?

Wonder Books produced a sequel of sorts with *Baby's First Christmas* (1959), examining most of the same activities through the perspective of a toddler. In the illustrations that accompany the extremely simple text, that youngster shows all the signs of being a child prodigy. If this were his first Christmas, he would have to be less than a year old, yet this kid is shown walking, playing with a toy train, riding a rocking horse, and during Christmas dinner, waving a turkey drumstick like a junior Colonel Sanders. And you thought kids grow up faster these days than they used to.

It was somewhat difficult for authors to come up with many variations on these plots. After all, there are only so many ways to tell the Nativity story or describe what happens leading up to Christmas. It was considerably easier to find new adventures for Santa Claus, since his one-note personality was such a blank slate that practically anything could happen in his stories. The real trick apparently was to keep Santa from being overshadowed by newly created friends and associates such as Rudolph and Uncle Mistletoe.

It seems that the old saying "familiarity breeds contempt" could be applied to Santa, as some of the authors sought to vary the stories by presenting the jolly old gent in his less-than-jolly moments. This brings us to Phyllis McGinley's 1956 book *The Year without a Santa Claus*. Even though McGinley later won a Pulitzer Prize for her poetic efforts, the only reason most people have ever heard of her Santa book today is that it was made into yet another of the Rankin/Bass holiday specials in 1974. The script of the TV show bears about as much resemblance to McGinley's book as the earlier Rudolph special did to Robert May's original verse; for example, Rankin/Bass and not McGinley created those well-

738

BABY'S FIRST Christmas

WONDER BOOKS WASHABLE COVERS

E. DART

Left: Baby's First Christmas *(1959) presented a remarkable tot who, though less than a year old, can walk, play with toys unsupervised, and eat roast turkey for dinner.* Below: *Phyllis McGinley, author of* The Year without a Santa Claus, *displays her Christmas tree decorated with kitchen utensils.*

remembered villains, the quarreling Miser Brothers Heat and Snow.

McGinley's story is told completely in rhyme, with some of the lines consisting of only one word. Santa decides that enough is enough and announces his intention to take Christmas as a day off for a change. After the world's initial shock, children from every country band together to bring presents to Santa, and their thoughtfulness impresses him so much that he cannot stand the thought of not making his annual journey. McGinley concludes:

> Though the great gale roars,
> Though nobody else would budge
> outdoors,
> Snug in your bed while the tempest
> drums
> You can count your blessings
> On fingers and thumbs,
> For yearly, newly,
> Faithfully, truly,
> Somehow
> Santa Claus
> ALWAYS COMES.

A similar situation occurred with Dr. Seuss's holiday classic *How the Grinch Stole Christmas!* (1957). Although the book had been a best-seller for nine years, it was only after famed cartoon director Chuck Jones turned it into an animated TV special in 1966 that the Grinch became a part of mainstream Christmas culture. As with Rankin/Bass's versions of Rudolph, Frosty, and *The Year without a Santa Claus*, when most people now think of the Grinch, they

Give a "GRINCH" for Christmas

Music and laughter and Yuletide fun galore in this Original TV Sound Track album. Starring Boris Karloff.

King Leo Records is a division of Metro-Goldwyn-Mayer Inc.

LEO THE LION RECORDS

KING LEO SERIES

LE/LES-901

THE ORIGINAL TV SOUND TRACK DR. SEUSS' HOW THE GRINCH STOLE CHRISTMAS NARRATED BY BORIS KARLOFF

Don't miss the TV premiere of "How the Grinch Stole Christmas" Sunday, Dec. 18-CBS-TV

Probably more people are familiar with Dr. Seuss's* How the Grinch Stole Christmas! *from the 1966 animated special than from the original 1957 book. For example, until the Grinch appeared on television, no one knew he was green.

remember elements that were created for the TV show. For example, in the book, all the illustrations were in black and white with red highlights. When production on the special began, one of the first decisions that had to be made was what color the Grinch should be. Jones recalled that Dr. Seuss originally insisted that the show be animated in the same black, white, and red style as the book, but somehow his artistic vision was overruled in this instance. The slimy shade of green that was eventually chosen for the Grinch's hide has become so familiar that some people probably believe he was green in the original book.

The Grinch made only one storybook appearance, but the "real" Santa just kept on turning up in volume after volume. In *Merry Christmas, Mr. Snowman* (Wonder Books, 1951), St. Nick takes pity on the title character, who has out of necessity been left in the yard and separated from the happy Christmas celebrations taking place indoors. When the children emerge from their snug and warm houses on Christmas morning, they find that Santa has left the snowman his furry red hat and used a stick to redraw the snowman's formerly frowning mouth into a smile. It is pure speculation as to whether Wonder Books rushed this story into production in order to capitalize on the big Frosty the Snowman publicity push of 1951.

The Happiest Christmas (Whitman, 1955) has perhaps the briefest text of any Yuletide tale, depending mostly on its illustra-

Santa Claus and his staff blast off into the Space Age in Rand McNally's* Santa's Rocket Sleigh *(1957).

tions to carry the plot. When the reindeer Blitzen goes missing one Christmas Eve, Santa soldiers onward with the remaining seven antlered quadrupeds, but the decrease in power causes sleigh, Santa, and deer to crash in the middle of the forest. The woodland animals see what has happened and pitch in to gather up the scattered toys and candy and restore the sleigh to working condition. Back at the North Pole, the contrite Blitzen shows up after all is said and done, and he is forgiven by the ever-forbearing Santa.

In *Santa's Rocket Sleigh* (Rand McNally, 1957), we are introduced to another of Santa's elfin helpers, this one known simply as Tiny Elf, along with his four brothers, Winkle, Tinkle, Clankle, and Bong. (We are left to wonder whether this quintet is in any way related to Snap, Crackle, and Pop.) Faced with the need to make his deliveries faster because of their increased numbers, Santa gives Tiny the job of coming up with a solution. Inspired by the sight of the toy rockets and jets in the workshop, Tiny devises rockets to be attached to the sleigh and reindeer harnesses to give the whole equipage the needed additional thrust. This is another story in which the reindeer are able to converse in English with Santa and the other North Pole inhabitants, a concept that seems to have depended on each author's preference.

One of the most unusual approaches was *Santa's Surprise Book* (Golden Books, 1966), which has even less of an actual plot than any of the ones mentioned above. In fact, the whole story line consists of Santa physically creating the book the reader is holding. On the last page, he jumps into the illustration on the first page, just so he can spend Christmas with everyone at the same time. Confused yet?

Because Clement C. Moore's poem *'Twas the Night before Christmas* entered the public domain too long ago to even talk about, publishers who needed something else to fill a gap in their Christmas titles could always be depended upon to bring it out in a new edition. The text remained generally the same, but it could be found illustrated in every conceivable style. Golden Books' 1949 edition was unique in that it emphasized the fact that the original verse was written in 1822 and thus depicted the people and events as they would have looked during that historical period. Most

What is the surprise in* Santa's Surprise Book *(1966)? That he spends the entire plot creating the book. Confusing, isn't it?

Since Clement C. Moore's poem* 'Twas the Night before Christmas *was in the public domain, publishers issued innumerable editions of it over the years. Little Golden Books' 1949 version (left) attempted to re-create a Christmas of the 1820s, when the verse was originally written, while Whitman's Tell-A-Tale retelling took a more modern approach.

others chose to assume the story took place in their own contemporary time frame and depicted Santa as either a giant, overweight man or a small, chubby dwarf, taking literally his description as a "jolly old elf." One thing about Santa that illustrators never could seem to agree on was how he looked with his hat off. Sometimes he was depicted as bald, while other times he had long, flowing white hair that matched his beard. Like his size and whether the reindeer could speak, this was strictly a matter of personal preference, it would seem.

Santa's Toy Shop *(1950) was among the first Christmas-themed Little Golden Books licensed by the Walt Disney Studios. It was very loosely based on a Depression-era theatrical cartoon.*

Golden Books enjoyed great success with its line of books based on the famous Walt Disney characters and movies. The authorship of most of them, including the Christmas titles, was credited to the ubiquitous—and nonexistent—Annie North Bedford. One of Golden's earliest combinations of Disney and Christmas had nothing to do with any of the studio's established characters, but appeared in 1950 as *Santa's Toy Shop*. It was a loose adaptation of a 1933 Disney theatrical short, *The Night before Christmas*. Santa is in one of his periodic bouts with self-pity, complaining because he is too busy to enjoy the many wonderful toys and other goodies being made in his workshop. He tells an unusually svelte Mrs. Claus, "Oh, jumping jacks! Now I have to give all these toys away, and I never will get to try any out!" Leave it to Mrs. C to solve the problem. She suggests that her hubby dash through his rounds as usual, until he has only one house left to visit, and then spend some leisure time playing with the toys. (She does not suggest what to tell the kids whose supposedly brand new toys have already been played with.)

Although Mickey Mouse justifiably remains the emblem of the entire Disney organization, in the 1940s and 1950s his popularity had somewhat slipped in favor of the more colorful and entertaining antics of Donald Duck and Goofy. Mickey makes only a brief appearance in *Donald Duck and Santa Claus* (1952), about the greedy duck's latest scheme to get more Christmas presents than anyone else in the world. He will accomplish this, according to his plan, by flying all over the earth in his supersonic airplane and leaving wish lists for Santa in every country, tailoring each to fit the local Christmas customs. He sets out wooden shoes to be filled in Holland, a sheaf of hay in Sweden, and so forth. Fortunately for Santa's gift supply, one of the elves stows away in Donald's plane and makes note of the whole nefarious plot. When Donald returns to the scenes of his crimes to collect his loot, he finds only switches or coal. When he returns home (his address is specified as Dopey Drive in Hollywood, the name of a thoroughfare inside the Disney studios), he finds a reasonable number of presents and a cautionary note from St. Nick, warning him that Santa is always watching. We do not see what sort of paranoid life Donald leads after this revelation.

Mickey, too, might have been a bit paranoid if he realized how his position as star Disney character was being usurped by the foul-tempered waterfowl. This was even more evident in Golden Books' *Donald Duck's Christmas Tree* (1954), which was a word-for-word retelling of the 1952 animated short *Pluto's Christmas Tree*, with

In **Donald Duck and Santa Claus** *(1952), the foul-tempered waterfowl tries to trick St. Nick into leaving presents for him in every country of the world.*

Donald taking the role Mickey had played in the original cartoon. This even extended to the point of the book showing Pluto as being Donald's pet dog rather than Mickey's. Unbeknownst to Donald, the live tree he cuts down and brings into the house happens to be the home of Chip 'n' Dale, the mischievous chipmunks. Pluto keeps trying to warn Donald that something is up (up the tree, that is), while the two rodents play with the lights and ornaments. When Donald finally discovers their presence, does he throw a dying duck fit? No sirree indeedy; he tells Pluto, "It's Christmas Eve. We must be kind to everyone. The spirit of Christmas is love, you know." Uh, wait a minute, wasn't Donald Duck here just a minute ago? Who is this sanctimonious soul who has taken his place?

Donald continued being one of the good guys in *Donald Duck and the Christmas Carol* (1960), notable because its illustrations were penciled by the inimitable Carl Barks of Disney comic book fame. The Christmas Eve revelry of Donald and his nephews is interrupted by a visit from miserly Uncle Scrooge McDuck, who wants them to drive him out into the countryside so he can bury the sacks of money he has accumulated through the year. When they refuse, Uncle Scrooge stamps off to his big, empty house, where he proclaims, "I don't care for anyone, and nobody cares for me— That's the way, if I had my say, that everyone would be!" Huey, Dewey, and Louie take turns dressing up as the ghosts of Christmas Past, Present, and Future and frighten the old skinflint into celebrating the holidays like everyone else.

Even when Mickey got his name in the title, he was often relegated to supporting-player status. Take the case of *Mickey Mouse Goes Christmas Shopping* (1953), in which he appears only at the beginning and end. The bulk of the story involves his nephews, Morty and Ferdy, and their adventures after accidentally being locked in a large department store after closing time. (Disney's third big star, Goofy, makes an unbilled cameo appearance as a store employee.) The two junior mice are taken back to Mickey and Minnie's loving arms by the store Santa, who is clearly identified throughout the text as "one of Santa's helpers" and not the real Mr. Claus.

Mickey finally got to be a star again, and barely missed meeting Santa in person, in *Mickey Mouse Flies the Christmas Mail* (1956). The resurgence of Mickey's status at this point was due to the recent television debut of the hit *Mickey Mouse Club*. Doing his usual good deed for the day, Mickey offers to help out the swamped postmaster by delivering the piles of holiday cards and letters, but his plane is blown off course dur-

ing a snowstorm, and he ends up making an emergency landing at the North Pole. The elves and Mrs. Claus are more than hospitable, but they have no gas to get the plane airborne again. Then Mrs. Claus remembers that they gave Santa a new sleigh as a Christmas present, and his old one is still parked outside. There are enough retired reindeer (illustrated as wearing nose spectacles and having white goatees) on the premises to pull the sleigh full of mail, so off Mickey goes on his errand of mercy.

The 1960 story *Donald Duck and the Christmas Carol* eventually came to play an important part in Disney history. It provided the inspiration for a 1975 album from Disneyland Records in which the famed studio characters dramatize the Dickens story. In the early 1980s, the animation staff decided to turn the record into a new animated featurette, which was touted as Mickey's first theatrical cartoon since 1953. *Mickey's Christmas Carol* was released in 1983 and naturally inspired its own tie-in Little Golden Book that year. There is not much point in rehashing the well-known story here, but Mickey, in the pivotal role of Bob Cratchit, finally got to shine once more. Donald Duck made only the briefest of appearances, but the meatiest part went to—you guessed it—Scrooge McDuck, recreating his original role of Scrooge. A more perfectly cast record, film, and Golden Book could hardly be imagined.

The Walt Disney Studios certainly did not have a monopoly on well-loved animated characters. Other studios were busy churning out cartoon hilarity of their own, and much of it spilled over into the same publishers' Christmas books. *Tom and Jerry's Merry Christmas* (Golden Books, 1954) was more or less patterned after the dueling duo's comic book series, which was being published during the same period; whereas the animated cartoons were done in pantomime, for the print media the pair was allowed to engage in dialogue. Their Christmas story starts out with the usual game of cat-and-mouse in full swing, with Jerry and his young friend Tuffy trying to swipe a meal from the Christmas dinner table, as Tom the cat does his best to keep them away. The ending takes a suitably sentimental twist, when instead of trying to capture and devour the mice, Tom leaves a miniature Christmas tree, loaded with goodies, outside their mouse hole.

The Terrytoons studio was responsible for *Mighty Mouse: Santa's Helper* (Wonder Books, 1955). This book was published at the same time the studio's cartoons were

finding a whole new life as one of the first Saturday morning shows, *Mighty Mouse Playhouse*. The story brings a crowd of the oddball figures together: Gathered for a Christmas party at Mighty Mouse's house are Gandy Goose, Dinky Duck, the Terry Bears, and Sylvester Fox. Santa's reindeer have all caught colds from playing in the snow, and the only one in relatively good health, Vixen, sends out an SOS for help. Naturally, the distress signal is picked up by Mighty Mouse's super hearing, and he takes all of his friends to the North Pole to help out. With the muscular mouse carrying the sleigh, the whole Terrytoons gang accompanies Santa on his rounds, and Christmas is saved once again. (Whew, it had me worried for a minute there!)

A crisis of a different sort rears its ugly head in *Howdy Doody and Santa Claus* (Golden Books, 1955). This time it is not the existence of Christmas that is threatened, but simply the happiness of Howdy Doody's pal Dilly Dally, who forgot to send a letter to Santa. Clarabell the clown, Inspector John J. Fadoozle, Chief Thunderthud, and the other TV show cast members are positive that Dilly is doomed to a holiday with no gifts, but it turns out that the freckle-faced and thoughtful Howdy wrote to Santa in Dilly's

Collectors of today can only gaze at the items in this Woolworth's ad, such as the* I Love Lucy *cut-out dolls, and weep over the prices. Oh, for a time machine . . .

stead. So all get what they most desire, and it is a happy Christmas in Doodyville. Although the story is credited to Edward Kean, Howdy's longtime TV writer, one has to wonder about the veracity of that claim. Remember the sexy Princess Summerfall Winterspring, as played on the tube by Judy Tyler? In this Golden Book, her name appears as Princess Summerspring Winterfall, a mistake that expert Kean would not likely have made. Kowabunga!

Dennis the Menace Waits for Santa Claus (Golden Books, 1961) was issued because of the popularity of the live-action television sitcom starring towheaded Jay North, but the book's illustrations are done in the style of the original Hank Ketcham comic strip, which illustrator Carl Memling did an incredible job of imitating. As one would expect, the plot involves the four-year-old terror's hyperactive pre-Christmas activities. After Dennis takes an ill-timed nap during the day on Christmas Eve, his harried parents fret that they will never be able to get him to sleep in order to put out his presents. As soon as it gets dark outside, however, the youngster yawns and asks to be tucked into bed, proving, as his mother puts it, "Anything can happen on the night before Christmas!"

At the same time that Dennis's escapades were entertaining both comic strip readers and TV watchers, the Hanna-Barbera animation studio had sprung seemingly out of nowhere to become the next big thing in cartoons. The fact that the studio's shows were produced on a fraction of the budget of a Disney film, and emphasized clever dialogue and voices over realistic movement, only helped make them stand out as something new. Just as Donald Duck and Goofy had pushed onetime superstar Mickey Mouse into the background, Walt Disney saw his entire cast being crowded out by the Hanna-Barbera menagerie in the late 1950s and early 1960s. This applied to the storybook world as well, so 1960 saw the publication of Golden Books' *Huckleberry Hound and the Christmas Sleigh.*

Perhaps because the characters were so much newer and less established than the Disney gang, Hanna-Barbera's tie-in merchandise could sometimes run at odds with the personalities given the characters for television. That is certainly true of this story, in which laid-back Huck Hound learns that mice Pixie and Dixie have never experienced an old-fashioned Christmas sleigh ride, and he sets out to rectify that. The inconsistent parts come when he enlists the help of Mr. Jinks the cat—who, under ordinary circumstances, "hated meeces to pieces"—and Yogi Bear, depicted as living on his own homestead, complete with large barn, rather than in the forests of Jellystone National Park. Thanks to the contributions of Jinks and Yogi, Huck fashions a sleigh out of an old baby carriage with skis attached to the bottom. Not until Christmas morning does he realize that he forgot about needing a horse to pull the sleigh, but Yogi comes to the rescue and takes Huck, Jinks, Pixie, and Dixie on a merry ride.

By the time of *Yogi Bear: A Christmas Visit* (Golden Books, 1961), the writers had gotten a better grip on the characters. During his breakfast of cereal (a subtle reference to the fact that all of the early Hanna-Barbera shows were sponsored by Kellogg's), Yogi receives a letter from his Uncle Northman Kodiak in Alaska: "Dear Nephew Yogi, we would all like to meet the only member of the family who is a televi-

sion star. Please come to visit us for Christmas." Yogi takes his Alaskan uncle at his word and, with little buddy Boo Boo, sets out for Kodiak Island. While getting a Christmas tree for the children, Yukon and Klondike, the adult bears run into a blinding snowstorm. Yogi's status as a Hollywood celebrity comes in handy, as he produces the sunglasses that all big stars wear in public, enabling him to see well enough to get them all back home safely.

Things were even more true to character in *Yogi Bear Helps Santa* (Whitman, 1962), which reads almost like the script of a cartoon, right down to Yogi's dialogue: "A nosy type hibernating bear like me has to keep an eye on things around Christmas time." Yogi intercepts Santa's visit to Jellystone Park and learns that the bearded gent has a present for everyone except Ranger Smith. "He's my problem too," admits Yogi, but he calls up his nemesis on the phone and imitates Santa's voice, asking the ranger what he wants for Christmas. The ranger isn't taken in and craftily replies that his number one wish is a summer without Yogi Bear bothering the tourists. "I am afraid that is impossible, sir," gulps Santa Yogi. "Do you have a number two wish?"

The ranger finally asks for a pair of jet-propelled skis so he can keep track of Yogi, and Santa tells Yogi that his elves have been working on just such an invention. While Santa naps in Yogi's cave, the green-hatted bear takes the sleigh and reindeer back to the North Pole and attempts to get back to Jellystone on the skis. He doesn't help his standing with the authorities any when his crash landing shatters Ranger Smith's Christmas tree into several thousand pieces. The story ends with the ranger chasing Yogi into the distance, angrily waving a broken ski in the general direction of the bear's skull.

All of these famous characters, plus many more, could also be found celebrating the holidays in issues of their comic books. There were considerably more Christmas-themed comics than one might think, probably because the publishers had to keep up a certain publication schedule, and it was just as easy to put out a Christmas issue as the last one of each year. This did not apply to all comic book series, however; for example, the much-loved Popeye comic books apparently never made reference to Christmas in the stories or cover art during the nearly forty years of their run.

Although Santa Claus could be counted on to make an appearance at any time and place in any other series, he was the undisputed star of *Santa Claus Funnies*, which Dell Comics published annually for twenty years. When this series is remembered at all today, it is because so many of the early stories were written and drawn by the incomparable Walt Kelly, who was then between his two more famous jobs as Disney animator and creator of the famed *Pogo* comic strip. Although *Pogo* justifiably became renowned for its biting social and political satire, Kelly's comic book work proved that such humor was only one facet of his talent. His stories for *Santa Claus Funnies* managed to be cute and funny at the same time, when the two concepts do not always work hand in hand.

In "How Santa Got His Red Suit," Kelly begins by explaining that at one time, Santa wore any color suit that suited him. The story gets under way with cranky Jack Frost hijacking Santa's sleigh and reindeer for a joyride, leaving St. Nick stranded in the forest. He takes refuge in the home of

Left: *Countless Christmas-themed coloring books were published over the decades; this particular one from the Samuel Lowe Company had a cover design identical to several of the late-1950s records on the Peter Pan label.* Above: *The great Walt Kelly, of later* Pogo *comic strip fame, showed his more whimsical side in a series of Dell comic books in the 1940s.*

some tiny elves, whose dialogue certainly foreshadows some of the inane attempts at conversation that would later enliven *Pogo*:

> FIRST ELF: Hooray! He's in!
> SECOND ELF: Who's in?
> THIRD ELF: Yes, who is he? Now that he's inside.

Dell published* Santa Claus Funnies *annually from the early 1940s to the early 1960s.

> FIRST ELF: Folks in here all want to know who you are—who are you?
> SANTA: Who am I?!
> THIRD ELF: You mean you don't know either?

Soon enough, Santa explains his predicament, and the elves not only get to work making new toys to replace the lost ones, but also call on their friend Timbertop the Giant to loan them the tail of his bright red coat. The elves reason that with such a distinctive new outfit, Santa will never have to worry about anyone not knowing who he is. "Everybody looks good in red—Besides, you'll look better in red than you will in nothing."

"The Great Three-Flavored Blizzard" (1947) opens with Fuzzychin the elf discovering the Easter Bunny painting eggs a few days before Christmas. The unusually springlike weather has fooled the rabbit into thinking it is time for his own holiday, and soon the duo finds that the weatherman (who, of course, controls all the weather) has run out of the necessary supplies to make snow. Santa and the elves get to work and load up the snowmaking apparatus with the ingredients for making ice cream, causing people no end of astonishment when their yards are covered in snow flavored vanilla, strawberry, chocolate, and (in Ireland, naturally) pistachio. As the Easter Bunny puts it, "Just think! Christmas sundae came on Thursday!"

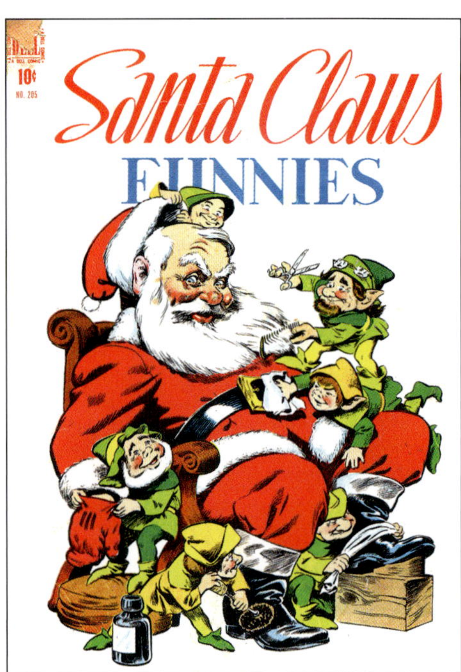

The cover art for* Santa Claus Funnies *varied from year to year. In this one, Santa looks more frightening than jolly. Scary Christmas, kids!

Not all of the stories in *Santa Claus Funnies* were the work of Kelly and his sense of humor. Dell editor Oskar Lebeck was credited with some of the scripts, including "A Letter to Santa" (1947). Told in the form of illustrations with text printed underneath, the story concerns a letter than upsets old Santa greatly. It is from a doll and a teddy bear he delivered the previous

Christmas, warning him not to bring any more toys to that particular child, because they have been terribly abused over the last twelve months. Santa finds the doll with most of her hair torn out and one arm missing, while most of the bear's stuffing has been shifted to his legs, so he can hardly stand. Acting on Santa's instructions, the reindeer Blitzen and an elf named Mr. Trundle see to it that the maltreated toys are repaired and given to a pair of children in a convalescent hospital. We never see what becomes of their ingrate of a former owner, whose page in Santa's book is marked, "No toys until further notice."

Apparently neither Lebeck nor Kelly was involved with "Santa's New Suits" (1948), which in some ways is the opposite of Kelly's suit origin story of a few years before. This time, Santa's elfin tailor, Nimble Needle, suggests that as a break from the normal routine, Santa should ditch the red suit and wear an outfit native to each country he visits. Santa dubiously agrees to try it out, but to the surprise of them both, instead of welcoming Santa as a fellow countryman, the residents of England, Scotland, Holland, Switzerland, and the rest mistake him for a local ne'er-do-well out to break into homes at night. As Christmas Eve wears on, Santa becomes less and less like

At one time or another, most of the well-known cartoon characters celebrated Christmas in issues of their comic books.

jolly old St. Nick and more like grumpy Old Nick: "That's the last suggestion you'll make, Nimble! One more and I'll feed you to my reindeer!"

For those who are fans of a certain genre of movie, the plot of "Christmas Comes to Mars" (1955) might sound a bit familiar. Two Martian youngsters, Tam and Teena, arrive on Earth via flying saucer on Christmas Eve. They are much impressed with all the joy and goodwill they observe but are particularly fascinated by the concept of Santa. Traveling to the North Pole at warp speed, they try to persuade Santa to return to Mars with them to make the children there happy, but this he admits he cannot do. Instead, he gives them one of his extra suits and a book on Christmas customs and sends them on their way. "Perhaps the time will come when Christmas will be celebrated throughout the universe," he philosophizes. And indeed, in 1964, that masterpiece of film schlock called *Santa Claus Conquers the Martians* explored just what happens when the aliens really do abduct Santa to entertain the green kids of their own planet.

Christmas in Disneyland ***(1957) used the framing story of Santa guiding two children through Walt Disney's Magic Kingdom to present unrelated adventures of Donald, Mickey, Goofy, and the rest of the gang.***

As many books as there were that featured the Disney character crowd celebrating Christmas, fans could find an even greater number of Disney-themed Christmas comics. There were many series of Disney comics on the market, ensuring Christmas stories aplenty during the last months of the year.

It has been well documented that Uncle Scrooge McDuck was introduced in Carl Barks's story "Christmas on Bear Mountain" (1947), in the Donald Duck series. Originally resembling his namesake literary predecessor, Scrooge soon became one of the comic books' most popular figures. His adventures were a year-round project, but whenever Christmas rolled around, he could usually be found "Bah, humbugging" it with the worst of them or engaging in outlandish competitions with nephew Donald to prove who could buy Huey, Dewey, and Louie more toys they didn't need.

In the late 1940s and well into the 1950s, the regular Disney comics line was supplemented with "giant size" (meaning they sold for the extravagant price of a quarter) special issues with titles such as *Walt Disney's Christmas Parade*. These issues included holiday stories involving many different characters, some from the Mickey-Donald universe, and others from the seemingly endless world of Disney feature films. This was also true of *Christmas in Disneyland* (1957), which unfolded an assortment of tales against the theme park background.

The book contains a running story of two siblings, Taffy and Timmie, who leave a note for Santa saying that their greatest wish for Christmas is to go to Disneyland. He instantly transports them there in his sleigh, and while sampling the various attractions, Santa introduces a story that is (sometimes very loosely) connected with each one. Sailing down the river in Adventureland's Jungle Cruise, Santa begins, "Well, Donald and his nephews were sailing to an island in the South Seas shortly before Christmas one year," and leads into yet another eighteen-page adventure precipitated by Uncle Scrooge's desire to load up on rare and valuable black pearls. In Frontierland, Santa goes off to deliver presents at the Indian tepees and leaves Taffy and Timmie to read a comic book that fell out of his bag, *The Iron Horse to Lonesome Gulch*, starring Mickey Mouse and Goofy. One of the weaker lead-ins comes when Santa and the kids take a spin on the rocket-ship ride in Tomorrowland and find some acorns on the seat, reminding Santa that Chip 'n' Dale live nearby. This cues another story in which the chipmunks rescue their pal Jiminy Cricket from villainous Brer Bear, who is determined to learn enough about Santa Claus to get the position for himself so he can devour the goodies people set out as a welcome for their visitor. One can almost hear Cliff Edwards's voice delivering the dialogue as Jiminy confides to Chip 'n' Dale, "At the rate old Brer Bone-Dome learns, I'll be here till the Fourth of July!"

Once that story is finished, the Disneyland tourists head for the Skyway ride, where Santa tells about Scamp, the young son of Lady and the Tramp, who decides that keeping out of trouble will be his Christmas gift to his parents. Finally, Santa and the kids end up in Fantasyland, where one story involves the single time the Big Bad Wolf did a good deed, by inadvertently using his newest Three Pigs-catching apparatus to find Brer Bear's children, who are lost in a snowstorm. Other tales are inspired by the Peter Pan and Snow White dark rides: Peter has to rescue Santa from the clutches of the greedy Captain Hook, and six of the Seven Dwarfs knock themselves sillier than they already are by trying to help Dopey perform a good deed and get on Santa's gift list. With Christmas-themed games and puzzles rounding out the pages, this book was a jolly Christmas treat in 1957 and is filled with nostalgia for us old fogeys of the twenty-first century.

Outside of the world of Disney, the Warner Bros. equivalent to such omnibus volumes was *Bugs Bunny's Christmas Funnies*, first issued in 1950. Like the Disney books, each year's looney installment featured an assortment of adventures with the cartoon studio's roster of stars, although there was usually no connecting story line to tie them all together. One typical example was "Santa's Black Beard"

Bugs "Santa" Bunny drops in on his fellow Looney Tunes stars on the back cover of* Bugs Bunny's Christmas Funnies *(1954).
DONNIE PITCHFORD

(1951), in which Bugs Bunny learns that Santa is determined to have his hair and beard dyed black so as to look younger and more vigorous. Bugs takes it upon himself to convince Mr. Claus not to tamper with his established image, and does so by mixing up a toxic tincture containing tar, glue, and other unappetizing substances. When all else fails, Bugs gets desperate and has the telephone operator connect him with every child in the world, all at the same time. Their unified scream, "DON'T DO IT, SANTA!" does the trick, and Santa retains his snowy white hirsute appendage.

The tiny tot terror Dennis the Menace had a long run in the comic book field, with his Christmas installments the highlights of any year. A running gag developed in these comics, involving Dennis's annual perusal of the mail-order catalog from "that big department store in Texas, Dieman-Harcus in Dallas." Seemingly each holiday season found Dennis requesting—and sometimes getting—the most outlandish presents imaginable from the semifictional catalog, to the extent that the store executives recognized the family name when an order arrived in the mail.

Dennis's penchant for causing trouble made the simplest holiday task a chore. In "Window Wonderland" (1964), dad Henry decides to create a display for their home's front window by cutting the letters for "NOEL" out of colored cellophane and taping them to the glass for a stained-glass effect:

DENNIS (wrapping himself in cellophane): Look, Dad! I turned blue!

HENRY: You'll turn BLACK and blue if you don't . . .

ALICE: HENRY! It's CHRISTMAS!

But Dennis could just as unwittingly become an agent for good. In "What's the Diff?" (1965), he stands up to a grouch who criticizes the work being done by the UNICEF Christmas fund.

The annual Christmas issue of the Dennis the Menace comic book usually featured the terrible tot trying to order outlandish merchandise from "that big store in Dallas, Dieman-Harcus."

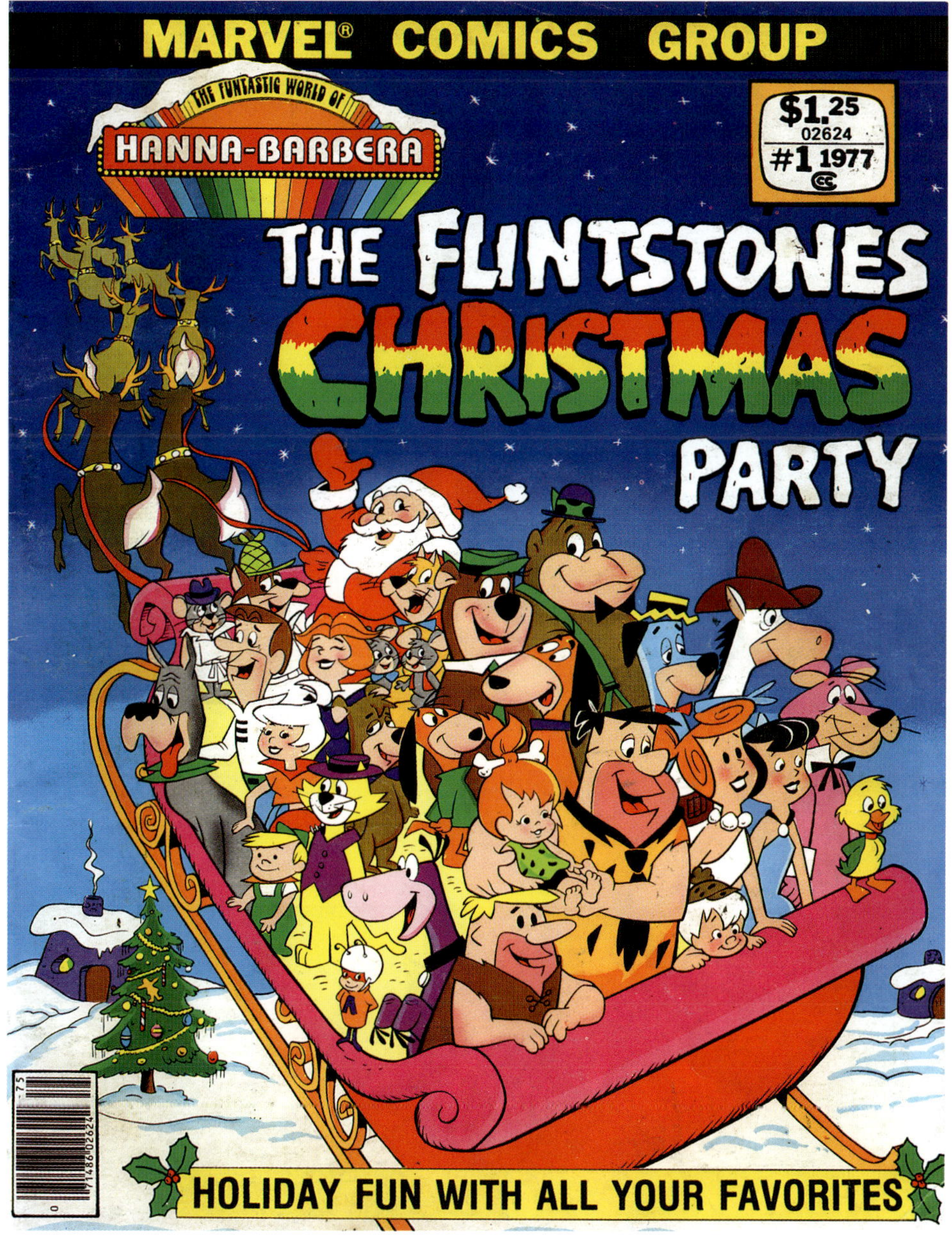

DENNIS: Yeah, Mister . . . they're tryin' to help some hungry kids! Don't ya LIKE kids?

GROUCH: Not NOSEY kids!

DENNIS: As long as they're helpin' kids that are hungry an' sick, what's the diff WHERE they sell their cards?

An appreciative crowd gathered on the city sidewalks takes up his refrain of "What's the diff?" until the old crab is forced to retreat, and Dennis gets his picture on the front page of the newspaper.

As for the vast Hanna-Barbera cast, their comic books had gone through several different publishers: first Dell, then Gold Key, and in the 1970s, Charlton Comics. Later in that decade, the rights to the characters were obtained by Marvel Comics, which set out to reinvigorate the motley crew in a big way. For the holiday season of 1977, Marvel issued an oversize comic book titled *The Flintstones Christmas Party*.

All right, you smarty-pants cartoon fans out there—we know what you're thinking, and you're not the first to come up with it. How, you ask, could the Flintstones celebrate Christmas when they live in prehistoric days, millennia before the birth of

How, you ask, could the Flintstones possibly travel through time and space to celebrate Christmas with the rest of the Hanna-Barbera cast? Good question! Does anyone have a good answer?

Christ? Well, it seems that as the years went by, the Hanna-Barbera writers and artists began to wonder the same thing, especially when it became necessary to have Fred, Barney, and the gang interact with Yogi, Huck, and their friends. Evidence, as in the form of this 1977 comic book, would seem to indicate that the town of Bedrock was not in the Stone Age timewise, but existed in some unspecified locale where time had stood still. Is that good enough for you? It had better be, because that is the only way to explain the concepts that follow.

In *The Flintstones Christmas Party*, Fred borrows money from the Krass Loan Company to buy toys for the Bedrock orphanage, only to learn that the fine print allows the shady outfit to take over the Flintstone home. Watching the action, Santa Claus determines to reward Fred for his unselfish deed and spends the rest of the book rounding up the other Hanna-Barbera characters to make a Christmas party to end all Christmas parties. The comic book includes individual stories centered around Yogi Bear, Super Snooper and Blabber Mouse, Huckleberry Hound and Quick Draw McGraw, Top Cat, Augie Doggie, and the Jetsons, each ending with the starring characters receiving an invitation to the Flintstones' party in Bedrock. To increase the guest list, there are also cameo appearances by Snagglepuss, Peter Potamus, Wally Gator, Hokey Wolf, Magilla Gorilla, Lippy the Lion and Hardy Har Har, Atom Ant, Pixie and Dixie with Mr. Jinks, and Touché Turtle. Just as they all gather for a big farewell party for the Flintstone home, the orphans announce that they have won first prize in a decorating contest, and they want Fred to use the money to pay back the loan on his house. The Krass Loan Company agent isn't anxious to comply until Magilla Gorilla and Lippy the Lion apply a little jungle justice, sending the crook screaming into the distance.

Reading about all of these favorite characters, plus the perennial Santa, Rudolph, and Frosty, was fine fun, but some youngsters preferred listening to them instead. This is where Christmas records come into the picture, so now, after a few seconds of needle scratch while you turn the page, we shall listen for ourselves. Say, do you hear what I hear?

Sing A KRIS KRINGLE JINGLE

Okay, you young people, it's time for a history lesson. When your elders (that's us) were your age, what did we do when we wanted to listen to music? No, we didn't have CDs, because those shiny little disks hadn't been invented yet. We listened to things called records. "And what were those?" you ask, trying to pretend you're remotely interested. Well, kiddies, records were flat pieces of vinyl or plastic that looked something like pizzas with holes in the middle. We listened to them by placing them on a bulky device called a record player, where the disks spun around and around while a sharp needle brought out the sounds that were embedded in their grooves. That, in a word, is why we thought they were so groovy!

As strange as it may seem today, when these devices are nostalgia pieces and museum displays, there was a time when records were new and the very idea seemed novel. In fact, it may surprise some people to learn that the first phonograph records were *not* the familiar-to-us flat disks, but round cylinders somewhat resembling the cardboard core inside a roll of toilet paper.

It would probably be impossible to point out with any certainty the very first Christmas carol or hymn to be immortalized in recorded form, whether on cylinder or disk. There were so many public-domain tunes—from the familiar "Silent Night" and "It Came upon the Midnight Clear" to even older medieval melodies—that producing them for records required little but an appropriate choir or soloist and some sort of musical accompaniment (or lacking that, they could be done in a cappella style).

One of the first original Christmas productions was not a song at all, but a pair of monologues launched in the December 1920 release list from Victor Records. The cat-

alog said of the routines' star performer, "Older Victrola lovers know Gilbert Girard. He is coming back, full of Christmas cheer, after a long absence," so it is anyone's guess whether he had done this type of material before. Side A of his highly touted release was "Santa Claus Tells about His Toy Shop," prompting this catalog description:

> Santa Claus arrives in a jangle of sleighbells and a clatter of reindeer hoofs. The louder the wind shrieks in the upper air, the louder Santa Claus laughs. He tells the children of his toy shop in the frozen North, entered through a door in an iceberg, and filled with the living animals from which he and his men model their Christmas toys.

Side B continues the story in "Santa Claus Gives Away His Toys." The synopsis:

> He takes the children on a sleigh ride through the air to see how presents are given out. They knock over a chimney, pass a steamboat and a motor car, beating them easily, then slip down a chimney into a household where the gifts are brought forth.

Remember these? This is a record player, and those are the records we used to play on it. Notice the distinctive red, blue, and yellow color scheme of the Cricket Records label.

A Special List of Christmas Records

Title		Artist	No.	Size	List Price
Cantique de Noël (Adam) *French*		Enrico Caruso	88561	12	$1.75
Silent Night, Holy Night		Gluck-Reimers	87544	10	1.50
Adeste Fideles (with Male Chorus) *Latin*		John McCormack	74436	12	1.75
Holy Night (Cantique de Noël) (with Lyric Qt.)	**Silent Night, Holy Night**	Lucy Marsh / Trinity Choir	45145	10	1.00
Angels from the Realms of Glory	**Oh, Little Town of Bethlehem**	Trinity Choir / Trinity Choir	35594	12	1.35
Night Before Christmas—Recitation	**Gingerbread Boy**—Recitation	Patten / Faulkner	35418	12	1.35
While Shepherds Watched	**It Came Upon the Midnight Clear**	Victor Oratorio Chorus / Victor Oratorio Chorus	35412	12	1.35
In a Clock Store	**Hunt in the Black Forest**	Victor Orchestra / Victor Orchestra	35324	12	1.35
Silent Night, Holy Night	**Christmas Hymns**—Selection *Harp*	Neapolitan Trio / Francis Lapitino	18389	10	.85
Silent Night	**Hark! the Herald Angels Sing**	Elsie Baker / Trinity Choir	17164	10	.85
Adeste Fideles (with Chimes)	**Joy to the World**	Trinity Choir / Trinity Choir	16996	10	.85
Christmas Morning at Clancey's	**Clancey's Wooden Wedding**	Steve Porter / Steve Porter	16936	10	.85

5247—IHUOIQ—10-12-20 VICTOR TALKING MACHINE COMPANY, CAMDEN, NEW JERSEY, PRINTED OCTOBER, 1920

Gilbert Girard's Santa escapades were apparently the model for a similar production intriguingly titled "Santa Claus Hides in Your Phonograph." There were at least two different versions of this concept, both of which have become legendary among record collectors. Each took advantage of the relative newness of phonographs and records, which no doubt still possessed a certain aura of mystery for the younger members of the household. Harry Humphrey narrated the earlier Santa record in 1922; the other, coming about a year later, featured the voice of Ernie Hare, a popular radio comedian of the era and half of the comic duo billed as the Happiness Boys. The Humphrey and Hare recordings used almost the same script, except that Humphrey's was done with Santa speaking in rhyme for the most part; Hare's version took the same phrases and turned them into prose.

Either one of them presents a very strange version of Santa to today's ears. Humphrey, especially, has an odd way of expressing Santa's famous "Ho ho ho" chuckle, making his laugh sound more evil than jolly. Hare's naturally deep voice gives much the same impression, although (thankfully) he does not laugh as much. Both begin with a knocking sound from inside the phono-

This Victor Records release list for December 1920 shows the mostly standard Christmas carols that were available at that time.

graph, and Santa calling out to the children in the room to close all the doors and windows before he will reveal his identity. (After hearing that voice and laugh, any kids willing to lock themselves in the room with it must have been in dire need of remedial *Romper Room*.)

"Santa Claus Is Comin' to Town," published in 1934, could be considered the beginning of the era in which Christmas songs became popular music in addition to sacred hymns.

As an example of the similar but differing approaches to the same material, here is the section of the Humphrey version in which Santa describes why he is not fit for the youngsters to see him just then:

My beautiful whiskers are black with the dirt,
And the dust's in my eyes so that both of them hurt;
And my lovely red robe with its trimming of white
Is as black as the black of a black winter's night!
(Evil laugh)
And it's all because I have to climb down
The many long chimneys you have in this town;
Before I can possibly come out and greet you,
I have to take a warm bath—and then perhaps I can meet you.

Now here is how Hare approached the same subject:

All night long, I've been climbing in and out of chimneys, leaving toys and candy and, oh, such wonderful presents for all the little folk. My whiskers are full of soot, and my beautiful red robe with its trimming of white is as black as black can be. I didn't want you to see me looking like that, so when I heard you coming, I hid in this phonograph!

Everyone had to get in on Santa's act in the mid-1930s. This 1935 sheet music features children's radio host Uncle Don, who was the forerunner of every local kidshow host on radio or television since.

Either case refutes the often-heard claim that it was the Coca-Cola ad campaign featuring Santa that first established his red and white suit to match the corporate logo. The famous Coke ads did not begin until 1931, long after these two evilly chuckling Santas had made reference to the color of their outfits.

All right, let's admit it—these early 1920s attempts at Christmas records seem as odd to us baby boomers as our childhood does to today's young people. The fact is that most of what we associate with our favorite Christmas records did not come along until after World War II. Oh, "Santa Claus Is Comin' to Town" first appeared in 1934, but it originally had a little touch of irony in that it seemed to reflect an impossible dream for those struggling with the Great Depression at the time. "White Christmas" was a product of the war and debuted in 1942, when servicemen stationed all over the globe could only dream of being able to celebrate Christmas as they used to. But with a few other exceptions similar to these, the big explosion of Christmas songs—especially those aimed at kids—did not take place until the period of postwar prosperity and the glut of new children it produced.

Gene Autry's "Rudolph the Red-Nosed Reindeer" was a red-nosed runaway hit in 1949 and inspired numerous other songs about newly created Christmas figures. At the same time that Columbia Records was enjoying the first wave of Rudolph's musical popularity, some of the companies that spe-

The Little Golden Records Christmas series from 1952 was promoted in this Woolworth's advertisement. Also notice the set of disks from Disney's soon-to-be-released* Peter Pan, *including one with the erroneous title "Second Star to the Left."

cialized in nothing but children's records were discovering their own niches in the holiday market. Of the major children's record labels, Little Golden Records and Peter Pan Records produced the majority of Christmas material, with Cricket Records and (in the late 1950s) Disneyland Records adding their own unique touches.

Golden Records, as you will no doubt recall from your childhood, were made of yellow plastic and originally came in only one speed, 78 rpm. Later, 45 rpm versions of the same songs were introduced, pressed in the more typical black plastic. Golden's output of the late 1940s through the 1950s had its own identifiable sound, as most of the records featured the solo voices of Anne Lloyd and Mike Stewart, with backup by a male vocal group called the Sandpipers. (This was not the same Sandpipers who had pop hits in the 1960s, including "Guantanamera" and "Cancion de Amor.") As far as the Christmas line, Golden mostly stuck with traditional songs rather than introducing originals. All the best-loved carols were represented, plus licensed hits such as "White Christmas." When Golden did de-

The Woolworth's/Golden Records Christmas lineup for 1953 had grown a bit over the previous year. Somehow they seem to have reversed the positions of "Mickey Mouse's Christmas Party" and "Mickey Mouse's Birthday Party." Mickey was quite a party animal back in those days.

cide to go outside the ordinary, it certainly produced some memorable moments.

No self-respecting children's record company would be caught without a version of "Rudolph the Red-Nosed Reindeer," and Golden respected itself enough to have at least two different versions. The Lloyd-Stewart one was as well done as all the rest, but when Golden came up with the idea of having Jimmy Durante perform the song in his own distinct style—well, let's just say the North Pole would never be the same again.

After a full chorus of the song, with Durante hamming it up along with the backup singers, he yells, "Stop da music!" so he can make a phone call to Santa. Durante reports that he has heard that Rudolph has been taking such good care of his health lately that his nose is not red anymore, "and I just wanted ta tell ya dat my soiveces are available." Soon enough, Durante learns that the reindeer have been out playing in the snow, and now not only Rudolph but also the other eight deer have red noses. "Ev'rybody wants ta get inta da act!" Durante shouts. Finally, after the song is over and done, he muses, "It just goes ta prove wot I always said—ya need a special kinda nose for a special kinda job!" The flip side had Durante talking his way through most of the lyrics of "Santa Claus Is Comin' to

These are just a few of the many Christmas titles offered by Little Golden Records over the years. BILL SMITH COLLECTION

Left: ***The great Jimmy Durante put his unique talents to work in this Golden Records pairing of "Rudolph" and "Santa Claus Is Comin' to Town."*** **Right:** ***Golden Records' version of "Frosty the Snow Man" gave the title character a voice for the first time, in the person of character actor J. Pat O'Malley.***

Town," but with little comedy dialogue to break it (and the listener) up.

If Golden was putting so much dependence on Rudolph, could Frosty be thumpety-thump-thumping far behind? No, indeed, and Golden might have gained the distinction of being the first company to actually give the jolly snowman a voice of his own. Side A of the disk featured the song performed by the Sandpipers, but on Side B, Frosty takes over with a deep voice supplied by J. Pat O'Malley. This character actor was just beginning his movie career at the time and would come to be a mainstay in Walt Disney films, both animated and live-action, for many more years.

At first Peter Pan Records followed much the same pattern as Golden, putting its stamp on holiday standards, with several different renditions of nearly every Christmas song in the company's catalog over the years. Occasionally something really stood out from the rest, such as one Peter Pan version of "Santa Claus Is Comin' to Town" that featured a Dixieland orchestra belting out the melody, leaving the definite impression that New Orleans was the town to which Santa Claus was comin'.

Another unique characteristic of the early Peter Pan Christmas records was that an actor playing Santa would narrate and introduce some of the age-old Christmas carols. Those who choose to believe that Santa was long ago divorced from the religious aspect of Christmas—and who think the well-known painting and sculpture of St. Nick kneeling at the manger is a recent and overdue concept—should give a listen to these mini-lectures. One of them runs like this:

> Whoa, Dancer! Whoa, Donder and Blitzen! Oh, ho ho ho! I'll bet you don't know who I am. You think you do? You think I'm Santa Claus? Oh, ho ho ho! You're right! I always come around at Christmastime, when everyone is singing:
>
> (CHOIR: "It Came upon the Midnight Clear")
>
> Midnight is usually the time I park my reindeer on the housetops and come down the chimney to fill good little boys' and girls' stockings with toys. Now you know why . . . because that was when the little boy Jesus was born. And say, do you know WHERE He was born?
>
> (CHOIR: "Away in a Manger")

Here is another example:

> This is Santa Claus, calling on all good little boys and girls to listen to the story of the very first Christmas—the first noel!

The back cover of the Peter Pan Records Christmas selections of the 1950s pretty much says it all. You probably remember staring at this ad while listening to the records, don't you?

In the 1950s, the cover art for Peter Pan Records varied widely from title to title, but all had that classic look that makes baby boomers' eyes moisten a bit. BILL SMITH COLLECTION

(CHOIR: "The First Noel")

When the little Christ child was born those many years ago, people all over the world were happy. The angels were so happy, they began to sing!

(CHOIR: "Hark, the Herald Angels Sing")

Well, I have to be getting back to my reindeer, so I can bring you good little boys and girls lots of toys! Up, Dancer! Up, Donder and Blitzen! Away!

When they did not feature Santa as a music commentator, most of the Peter Pan records were credited only to the Caroleers, a group of studio singers whose given names have been lost to history—even to those who currently run the company. One singer who did receive label credit repeatedly was Dick Edwards, whose name turns up on song after song, from "Rudolph" and "Frosty" to "Silent Night" and "I Heard the Bells on Christmas Day." Either Edwards recorded for Peter Pan for so many years that his voice deepened and mellowed, or else there was more than one male vocalist who used that name, because Edwards's alleged earlier recordings bear little resemblance to the later ones.

For a brief period, the paper sleeves for Peter Pan Records came with a hole that displayed the actual record label contained therein. The story is told that when someone remarked to Irving Berlin that "White Christmas" was the best song he ever wrote, Berlin responded, "It's the best song anybody ever wrote!"

Compared with Golden and Peter Pan, Cricket Records' Christmas offerings—at least so far as nonoriginal compositions were concerned—seem rather unimaginative. Most of the classic tunes were represented, but the only one to rise above the

Left: ***After Golden and Peter Pan, Cricket Records was the third-largest producer of children's Christmas tunes.*** **Right:** ***Even though "All I Want for Christmas Is My Two Front Teeth" was composed in 1946, the cover of Cricket Records' version of the song was firmly rooted in the 1960s school of design.***

ordinary was "Rudolph," for which Cricket somehow managed to get Gene Autry to record an entirely new performance of his signature song. There is no indication of what his usual label, Columbia, thought about that. Otherwise, Cricket's renditions were pretty standard.

One dubiously notable incident came in one of the company's at least two different renditions of Victor Herbert's classic ode to lost childhood, "Toyland." Whereas the original lyric contained the bittersweet closing line, "Once you pass its borders, you can never return again," Cricket's staff apparently felt this would be a bit too traumatic for young ears. The female soloist instead sings, "Once you pass its borders, you will surely return again," completely changing the intended meaning of the song. Cricket also modernized Herbert's "March of the Toys," adding lyrics that referred to toy "satellites, rockets and jets," which did not yet exist when the song was originally written in 1903.

The label issued a version of "All I Want for Christmas Is My Two Front Teeth" with an irresistibly bouncy beat, but the uncredited singer overemphasized the song's necessary lisp almost to the point of being unintelligible. Cricket also produced an abbreviated dramatization of "A Christmas Carol" that featured Scrooge receiving a visit from Marley and the three Christmas ghosts on four successive nights—which means, if the story began on Christmas Eve, Scrooge did not learn his lesson until it was far too late to do anything about celebrating the present holiday season.

The other labels had to bow their heads when it came to the sheer number of original Christmas tunes churned out by the tunesmiths at Peter Pan Records. In most cases, these never-before-heard productions were batched together on LPs headlined by one familiar song, such as "Santa Claus Is Comin' to Town" or "Snoopy's Christmas." Other than the lead-off song, everything else was new. The songs could also be mixed and matched endlessly on 45 rpm singles.

These Peter Pan originals have developed quite a following on the Internet, but very little is known about their creation. If you have always wondered who the performers and writers behind these Christmas classics were . . . you're just going to have

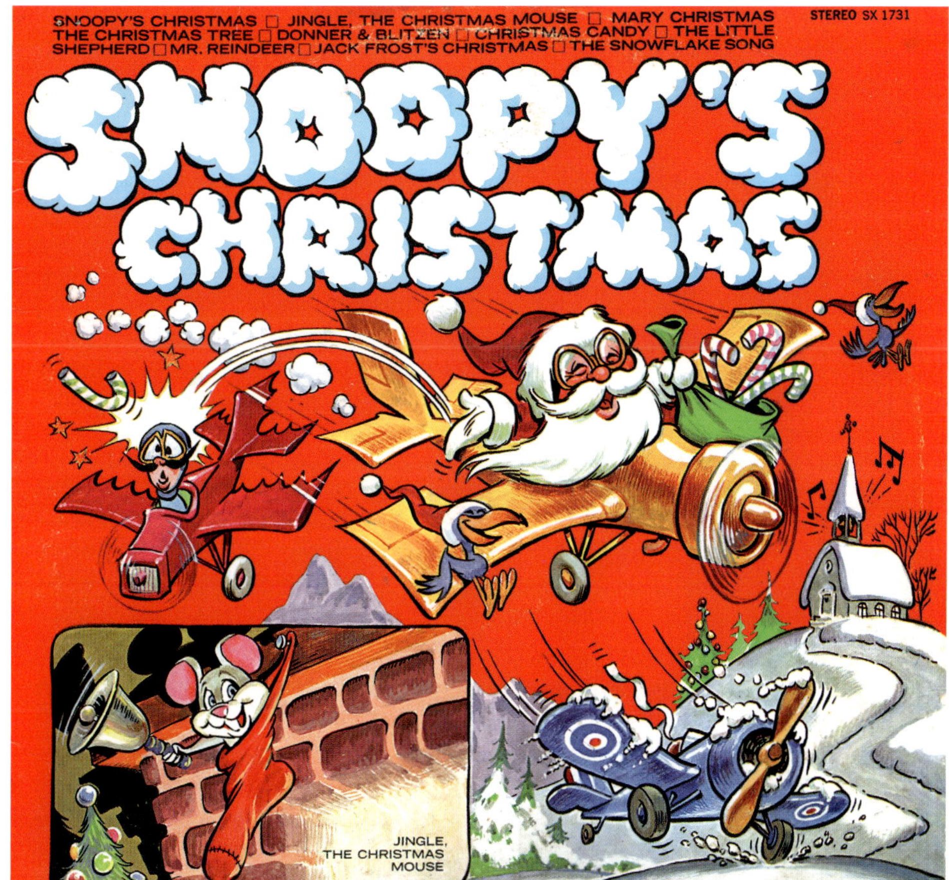

The cover of this Peter Pan Records LP was created by Howie Post, best known for his Harvey Comics work with such characters as Wendy the Good Little Witch. Here Post had the unenviable task of trying to illustrate "Snoopy's Christmas" without showing Charles Schulz's beagle anywhere in the picture.

to keep wondering. All attempts to learn the identity of anyone connected with these recordings have been met by the proverbial brick wall (which, in this case, even has snow on top and icicles hanging from it). The present-day incarnation of Peter Pan Records, known as Inspired Studios, apparently has kept no such information in its files, and those who would have had firsthand knowledge have long since gone to sing Christmas carols with that same heavenly host that performed for the shepherds near Bethlehem. Therefore, all we can do here is pick apart some of the best-remembered Peter Pan songs and get that same warm and fuzzy feeling we had when we drove our parents nuts by playing them over and over from October until January.

One thing that is fairly obvious from listening to the songs is that most of them featured the same trio of singers. One was a male vocalist with a deep baritone or bass voice, who was usually called upon to solo when Santa Claus was required to sing some lines, but who could also be assigned more unusual fare. For example, in "The Day before the Night before Christmas," our friend, whom we shall call Deepy, is supposed to be a little boy frantically trying to make up for the past year's transgressions in twenty-four hours. ("Cleaning up and brushing up and washing my ears / Hey, a day isn't long enough; it'll take years!")

Deepy was usually accompanied by two ladies with widely varying vocal stylings. One, whom we shall call Julie because that is how the other two refer to her in the song "Where Is Christmas?," had a beautiful, lyrical singing voice that was well suited to comparatively serious or sentimental material. The other tended more toward comedy, and we can call her Brat because so many of her songs required her to adopt that type of persona. One of her greatest performances was in "Who's That Up on the Roof?," which initially seems to set out to turn all previously established holiday hits on their stocking-capped heads:

> You can't fool me, oh no sirree,
> I'm not so dumb;
> That's Daddy in a Santa Claus suit
> Downstairs kissin' Mom.
> I know there is no Santa Claus,
> And now I've got the proof;
> But if that's Dad downstairs kissin'
>   Mom,
> Who's that up on the roof?

Deepy, Julie, and Brat stayed together through song after song, most of which were meant to be upbeat and humorous in some form. A notable exception was "Icicles, Holly, Red Berries and Snow," which gave a truly evocative portrait of spending Christmas Eve with those you love most. ("Ice cream and marshmallows, egg nog and then / Singing of peace and good will to all men / No wonder nobody wants this night to end.") But most of their efforts were aimed at getting a chuckle and sometimes made a pointed statement at the end.

Take, for example, "The Christmas Tree That Ran Away." Julie and Deepy sing the story, which concerns a "kind of scrawny, kind of thin" tree that has somehow come to be set up in a huge mansion. "On Christmas Eve, he heard the mistress of that big old house say, 'That little tree is ugly; get a new one right away,'" Deepy intones. Brat supplies the voice of the tree in each chorus, where the clinically depressed pine laments, "Nobody wants me and tomorrow's Christmas Day / Nobody wants me, I'm gonna run away." Trudging through the countryside with gifts dangling from his branches—and no doubt risking being caught for stealing such valuables from the mansion—the tree spies a "little cabin on the hill," where a small boy is saying his prayers: "We don't expect presents, God, but maybe you could see / Some way of getting us just a little Christmas tree." The unwanted tree crawls inside during the night, causing the poverty-stricken family to pronounce the event a miracle.

Another joint Deepy-Julie-Brat song is "The North Pole Express," which begins with the lyrics "Down at the station, lights all aglow / Eight reindeer and engine are ready to go / There she stands in the land of ice and snow/ (TRAIN WHISTLE) / The North Pole Express!" One cannot help but wonder if author-illustrator Chris Van Allsburg had heard his children playing this record prior

Left: ***Howie Post struck again with his "Santa Claus Is Comin' to Town" cover, graphically illustrating two of the original songs on the LP, "The Christmas Tree That Ran Away" and "Ten Thousand Santa Clauses."*** **Right:** ***Contrary to what one might expect, this Peter Pan LP did not contain renditions of the famous tunes "Sleigh Ride" and "Jingle Bells." Instead, the title track was a brand new composition actually titled "Sleigh Ride/Jingle Bells."***

to creating his renowned 1985 book *The Polar Express*. Brat got to solo again in "Ten Thousand Santa Clauses," in which she rants about the number of fake Santas prowling the landscape while she cannot enjoy any of them because of being laid up with the mumps.

Peter Pan's songs also served to introduce several new Christmas characters, none of whom made any impression outside of their particular melody. There is "Jingles, the Christmas Mouse," who spends the whole year practicing to be the "mouse who wasn't stirring" on the night before Christmas. "Mr. Reindeer" refers to a figure not previously documented in North Pole history: "He's a most important gent, and here's the reason why / All year long his time is spent teaching reindeer how to fly." Like the earlier Peter Pan version of "Santa Claus Is Comin' to Town," "Mr. Reindeer" explodes into a Dixieland jazz number just when no one is expecting it. A rather short ditty pays tribute to "Mary Christmas," an Eskimo girl who once lived next door to Santa and assured her place in history by teaching the elves how to make toys. And "Mama Santa's Surprise" has its own surprise ending, introducing yet another celebrity to the arctic roster:

> If you'd like to know what it's all about,
> Come up to Toyland and you'll find out,
> When you see everyone playing games
> and having fun
> With Rudolph Reindeer's brand-new
> son!

Coming a few years after the Deepy, Julie, and Brat productions was Peter Pan's series of albums starring the Peppermint Kandy Kids. Although the LPs generated a respectable number of never-before-heard songs, the main distinguishing feature of the Peppermint Kandy Kids was the astonishing variety of regional accents within the group. Some songs have young soloists with accents ranging from British to Brooklyn, while others feature adults doing character voices. Like the earlier originals, the Peppermint Kandy Kids productions were carved up and marketed as 45 rpm singles for years.

With all of this going on, Cricket Records knew when it was squashed. The company made only a few halfhearted attempts at

This cover from Cricket Records is a terrific example of art that shows something that has nothing to do with the song on the record. Who is that driving the sleigh anyway, Santa Claus Junior?

Although Walt Disney personally conceived the idea for Ludwig Mousensky and the All-Mouse Symphony, their 1957 debut Christmas record was not a hit.

original songs, and even they failed to chirp their best. "Mixie Pixie" was probably the nearest to what Peter Pan was doing, describing yet another of Santa's legions of helpers, whose particular responsibility was keeping Rudolph's nose shiny and bright. One Cricket song that really seemed to go nowhere was "Tinker Town Santa Claus," describing a burg with an unusual collective problem:

> Tinker Town folks are no different
>   from us
> But their voices they can't control;
> When Tinker Town folks all start
>   to sing,
> It sounds like they're standing in a hole.
> Next year, Santa, when you call
> Please bring us the wherewithal
> So we won't sound like we're a mole,
> Singing songs in a great big hole.

Uh, okay, if you say so. Now that we have spent more time in Tinker Town than we really wanted to, let's move along and talk about Disneyland Records' contributions to the season. If you want the complete story of how this legendary studio established its own in-house record label, I can without bias—okay, maybe not totally without—direct you to the book *Mouse Tracks: The Story of Walt Disney Records* (University Press of Mississippi, 2006), by Greg Ehrbar and, ahem, yours truly. It is not my intention to rehash that whole work here, but I will establish that Disneyland Records was founded in 1956 and go on from there.

For the second Christmas season of the company's existence, 1957, the main production would come to have far-reaching effects in not only Christmas records but the children's music world in general—only Disney would not benefit from it. It all started when Walt Disney approached the head of the company's record division, Jimmy Johnson, with an idea. This was relatively uncommon in itself, as Walt was normally so busy overseeing the many facets of his company that he rarely paid much attention to what was being done in the merchandising realm. His name was on it all, however, so when he did have a suggestion, or a command, his employees listened.

Walt's idea was to create a Christmas record using the same type of sped-up voices the studio had devised for the mice in *Cinderella* (1950). He explained to Johnson that this group of mice lived under the stairs at the studio, and the record company had discovered them and released the first production by "Ludwig Mousensky and the All-Mouse Orchestra." Johnson and his co-producer, Tutti Camarata, got to work to follow Walt's wishes as closely as possible.

The resulting record, "Walt Disney's Christmas Concert," satisfied nearly no one, including Walt, who groused that he had never known a musician who had a sense of humor. The sped-up voices used for the mice, including Jimmy Macdonald (who was then working regularly as the official voice of Mickey) putting on an atrociously bad Austrian accent as Ludwig Mousensky, were the only humorous thing about the production. Once that novelty wore off, there was little to hold a listener's attention. The mice did not tell jokes or engage in funny dialogue, and their songs tended toward the standard Christmas carols. "O Little Town of Bethlehem" hardly sounds its most inspiring when delivered by squeaky mice.

By the following Christmas season, 1958, Disneyland Records had forgotten about the Mousensky debacle and moved on to other things. Over at Liberty Records, however, the acorns were just beginning to fall. Actor-composer Ross Bagdasarian, whose previous big song hit had been Rosemary Clooney's "Come On-a My House," had been doing some playing around with vocal effects too. The advent of tape for mastering records had opened up new worlds of possibilities that did not previously exist, and one of these was the ability to record voices and music at one speed and play them back at another. This would give the effect of either raising or lowering the pitch of the voices, depending on which direction was taken.

The Mousensky record had been done this way, but in a rather complex manner. Producer Tutti Camarata once explained that the voices and music were recorded at one-third the speed at which they would later be heard. This meant that in the finished product, the music was pitched higher, just as the voices were, to make it sound more like mouse-size instruments being played. Bagdasarian had come up with a more basic way to handle voices; he recorded them at half speed. For example, for a finished tape that was to play at 15 inches per second (ips), the recording was done at 7½ ips. The musical backing was also slowed down to that speed, so when all was finished, the music sounded normal, but the vocals were shrill and squeaky.

Bagdasarian performed under the stage name of David Seville, and he first put his double-speed experiment to use in a song called "Witch Doctor." He sang the lyrics in his natural voice, then brought in his solo sped-up voice to represent the title character: "Oo-ee-oo-ah-ah, ting-tang-walla-walla-bing-bang." It went over so well with listeners that he decided to try singing three-part harmony with himself, using tape to dub his three performances on top of one another. Since the resulting sound made him think of how chipmunks might sing if they possessed the ability, he called his new creation "The Chipmunk Song" and named its three stars after some of his fellow workers at Liberty Records: Alvin, Simon, and Theodore.

"The Chipmunk Song," also known by its subtitle, "Christmas Don't Be Late," was the smash hit of the 1958 Christmas season. Featuring David Seville as the chipmunks'

A year after Disney's flop with the All-Mouse Symphony, songwriter Ross Bagdasarian (David Seville) got it right when he created Alvin and the Chipmunks. The cover on the left shows the trio's original, more realistic rodent appearance; the one on the right dates from after their final design was established for their prime-time cartoon series in 1961.

not-so-long-suffering authority figure and Alvin as the born troublemaker, the song presented all of the opportunities for comedy that were lacking in the Mousensky material. "The Chipmunk Song" not only began a pop culture phenomenon that continues even today, but also inspired (if it can be put so kindly) imitators among most other children's record companies. In just a moment, we will take a look askance at some of those and see how well they did or did not succeed in their goals.

Meanwhile, if the Chipmunks were becoming recording stars, could merchandising be far behind? Just as with the other Christmas characters that emerged from such a background, by the following season there were Chipmunk toys on every

The year after "The Chipmunk Song" made it big, Little Golden Books built* The Chipmunks' Merry Christmas *around the novelty tune. Notice that illustrator Richard Scarry made Alvin, Simon, and Theodore look more like squirrels than chipmunks.

store shelf. Little Golden Books, always able to smell a trend, came up with *The Chipmunks' Merry Christmas* (1959). It was illustrated by Richard Scarry, fresh off his work on the Rudolph Golden Book, but the artist seemed to have an easier time with dancing deer than with burrowing rodents. Before a standardized image for the Chipmunks was developed in 1961, the trio was depicted in any number of ways; Scarry's version was ultrarealistic but actually resembled squirrels more than chipmunks.

The text also reflected the problems inherent in trying to make a plot out of something that existed only as a novelty record. David Seville was absent from the story, and his role as taskmaster was assumed by one Mr. Owl. These lines from page 7 of the book demonstrate how the author tried hard to convey the spirit that had made "The Chipmunk Song" so popular:

> When they arrive at the burrow, Mr. Owl is waiting. It is time for the chipmunks' singing lesson.
>
> "Are you chipmunks ready to sing your song?" asks Mr. Owl.
>
> "Okay," says Simon.
>
> "Okay," says Theodore.
>
> "Alvin?" says Mr. Owl. No answer. "ALVIN!" shouts Mr. Owl.
>
> "OKAY!" Alvin shouts back.

While Alvin and the Chipmunks were laughing all the way to the nut bank during the 1958 holiday season, Disneyland Records was ignoring them and striking out in different directions. That year marked the debut of Disney's song "From All of Us to All of You," which would become the studio's semiannual Christmas theme. It was penned for that year's premiere of the television episode of the same name, but a different version was simultaneously produced by the record division. Like the TV rendition, the record was performed by Cliff Edwards as Jiminy Cricket, with some additional lines by Jimmy Macdonald, who supplied not only the voice of Mickey Mouse, but also that of Goofy.

Thanks to Little Golden Records, Disney was not about to let people forget that squeaky-voiced Chip 'n' Dale had come before either Ludwig Mousensky or Alvin and the Chipmunks.

The liner notes on "From All of Us to All of You" claimed that Mickey Mouse was "the only eight-fingered piano player in the world." A somewhat questionable lyric by Goofy, "I'll hang you on my Christmas tree, you'd be a pretty bangle," was deleted in later reissues of the song, as it didn't do much to support his usually harmless personality.

Disney's other big push for Christmas 1958 was a tie-in with *Family Circle* magazine. The December issue of that publication boasted a lavishly illustrated twelve-page feature titled "A Christmas Adventure in Disneyland." The accompanying verse was crafted by longtime Disney writer and story man Dick Huemer. It bore a light resemblance to the *Christmas in Disneyland* Dell comic book of the year before, as once again two twins—John and Jane, this time—are magically transported to the Magic Kingdom on Christmas Eve. Instead of being shown around by Santa Claus, here the kids are under the less psychologically stable care of Mr. Toad, who uses his questionable driving skills to get them from one Disney land to another and show them how the inhabitants of each celebrate Christmas.

The ending of the *Family Circle* feature plugged the fact that Disneyland Records

This Christmas 1958 issue of* Family Circle *was the origin of Dick Huemer's poem "A Christmas Adventure in Disneyland," which was later adapted for records.

had made available a 45 rpm disk called "Christmas Trees of Disneyland," with four songs based on Huemer's poem. In fact, even the songs featured lyrics by Huemer, with music composed by Tutti Camarata. One, called "Storybook Land Christmas Tree," describes lights composed of tiny, flittering sprites, "all personal friends of Tinker Bell." In the theme song for the Adventureland "Jungle Tree," usual enemies of the animal kingdom gather in peace around a tropical tree. It has an unusually reverent ending: "'Thy kingdom come,' I breathed in prayer, and silently stole away / All would be well on earth, I knew / All will be well someday."

The Tomorrowland "Futuristic Tree" is said to resemble a rocket ship with "fingers pointing at the moon." The stated moral of this minor-key and somewhat unsettling number is "A Christmas time there'll always be / There'll always be a Christmas tree." And the strangest tune of all centers around the tree found deep in the caverns of the Snow White dark ride in Fantasyland. "Jingle Bones" is cackled by Gloria Wood as the witch from that attraction, accompanied by two of her companion hags: "We're wearing holly wreaths on our pointed hats / Flying 'round our tree with our vampire bats." For the 1959 Christmas season, Huemer's complete poem received a Disneyland Records release, with these four songs incorporated in their proper places.

That was also the time when the other record labels—both children's and otherwise—decided that if the Chipmunks could do it, so could they. One of those companies was Capitol Records, which had already produced some tremendous hits in its children's line, including its own Bozo the Clown and records starring such licensed characters as Woody Woodpecker and the Looney Tunes crowd. For 1959, Capitol threw its antlers into the Chipmunk soundalike ring with its single "The Happy Reindeer," sung by a trio billed as Dancer, Prancer, and Nervous.

Those names might produce at least a chuckle today because of the incongruity of one of them, but listeners in 1959 would have immediately picked up on its origin. Over a musical vamp that strongly resembles the opening of "The Chipmunk Song," the reindeer introduce themselves. When the third one stutters and stumbles over his name, one of the others asks, "Say, are you nervous?" "Nope!" the doddery deer replies. Not exactly Bob Hope-quality humor there, but it was a takeoff on the routine performed by Don Knotts on television's *Steve Allen Show*. Each week, the trembling Knotts would be asked, "Are you nervous?" to which he would bark, "Nope!" with a terrified expression. Since it was funny for Knotts to look like a deer caught in the headlights, apparently Capitol felt it was acceptable for a real deer to lift the same gag.

The rest of "The Happy Reindeer" involves the three high-pitched voices singing simple lyrics: "We are Santa's reindeer / We've learned to sing this year / So we can tell everyone Christmas Day is near." No credits were issued for the song, so the identity of the singer (or singers) behind the sped-up reindeer voices is still a mystery.

Unlike the Chipmunks, Dancer, Prancer, and Nervous did not go on to have an illustrious multimedia career. Being reindeer, they were perhaps tied too closely to the Christmas season to be able to escape from it, as did Alvin and his brothers. It is known that the reindeer made a similar-sounding "Happy Birthday" record. Somehow Capitol arranged to have animation put to it, and the short music video became a staple of local children's programs in various TV markets. It still looked a bit odd to have natal day wishes extended by three cartoon reindeer wearing jingle bell-bedecked harnesses, but that's show business.

When Cricket Records decided to enter the squeaky sweepstakes, it did so with two distinctly different groups. "Santa's Helpers" appeared in a series of standard Christmas tunes, broadcast direct from the North Pole, it is assumed. Unlike the Happy Reindeer, Santa's Helpers came with their own equivalent to the Chipmunks' David Seville—none other than Santa Claus himself, although his dialogue was generally limited to lines such as "Say, do you fellows know 'Joy to the World'?" or "Now let's sing the most beloved Christmas carol of all, 'Silent Night.'" Yes, like the All-Mouse Orchestra, Santa's Helpers had no qualms about applying their style to

Left: ***Many other record companies felt that if the Chipmunks could do it, so could they. One of the more blatant sound-alikes was Santa's Helpers, who appeared on Cricket Records and various other subsidiary labels.*** **Right:** ***In addition to Santa's Helpers, Cricket Records aped the Chipmunks with—what else?—the Happy Crickets. Usually their voices were sped up, but in some of their songs, the performers simply sang in falsetto voices.***

what normally would have been deeply emotional or reverent melodies.

Cricket Records' second set of Chipmunk clones was known as—befitting the name of the label—the Happy Crickets. Their Christmas selections sounded about like all the others who had discovered the joys of recording at half speed, with one glaring exception: On their self-titled LP and various 45 rpm singles edited from it, the Happy Crickets sing in the same double-speed voices as the Chipmunks and Santa's Helpers—*except* when they perform "The Chipmunk Song." For that track only, rather than sped-up voices, the Happy Crickets are represented simply by singers using falsetto voices similar to that of Mickey Mouse or Mister Moose from the *Captain Kangaroo* show. Perhaps Cricket Records got six cold feet when it came to duplicating the Chipmunks' technique to re-create their own theme song.

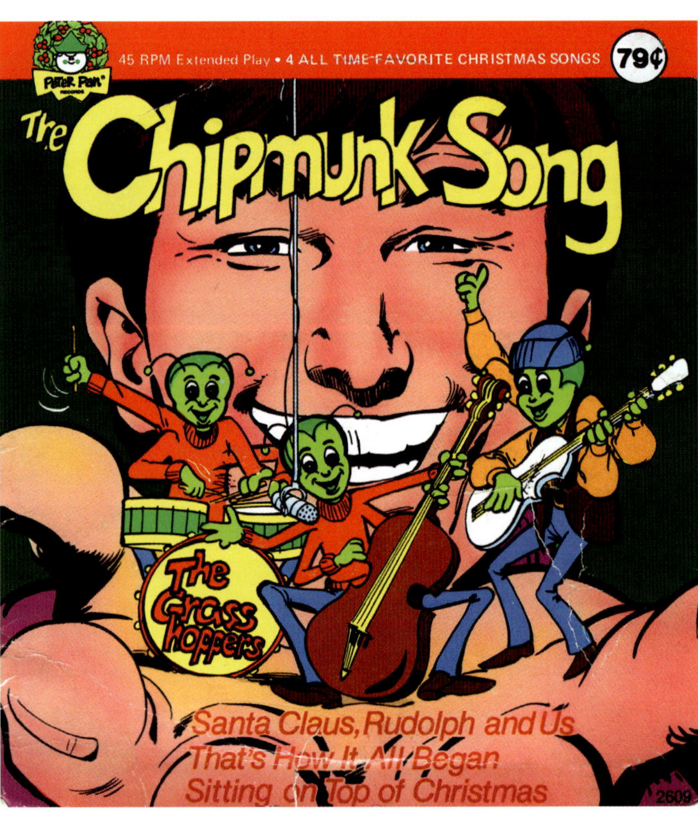

Left: ***Peter Pan Records introduced the Grasshoppers, Dennis, Archie, and Ricky, in 1959; their David Seville straight-man equivalent was Eddie Maynard.*** **Right:** ***The Grasshoppers were revived for another set of Christmas songs in the late 1960s, still getting under the skin of a substitute David Seville.***

The leader of all the Chipmunk cloners was Peter Pan Records. What was that company's group called, and what sort of creatures were they supposed to be? Those are very good questions, and if you can figure out the answers from the discussion below, you are doing better than all the other children's record historians put together.

Evidence, in the form of some of the earliest material released in 1959 as 78 rpm disks, would seem to indicate that the Peter Pan group was known as the Grasshoppers. Here their names were given as Dennis, Archie, and Ricky, with Dennis as the smart-aleck, trouble-prone Alvin equivalent. Like Santa's Helpers on the Cricket label, the Grasshoppers even had their own David

Seville parallel, originally credited on the label as Eddie Maynard, although it is not known whether Maynard tripled as the voices of all three Grasshoppers as well. As updatings of the recordings were done over the years, other "Dave" actors were brought in, and some records feature lines spoken by more than one "Dave" voice, even within the same song.

That's not the end of the story, however. Some of the Peter Pan 78s feature the same recordings, but with the singers billed as the Pixies. And one bizarre configuration from that period has a label boasting the Pixies billing, the record referring to the singers as grasshoppers, and the paper sleeve depicting three chipmunks. Now do you see why this is so complicated?

But wait, there's more! During the same Grasshoppers/Pixies era, still more Peter Pan singles had the same recordings, but with references to the group's name removed and billed on the label as "The Singing Mice: Eke, Zeke and Squeek." Confused yet? You haven't heard the end of this. Sometime in the late 1960s or early 1970s, judging from the changing musical style, the Grasshoppers were revived for a new set of songs. But from the same time frame, there are singles and LPs with the phony Dave Seville's introductions re-recorded to refer to the group as the Bunny Hoppers, with cartoon artwork of rabbits on the jackets. So was the Peter Pan equivalent of the Chipmunks the Grasshoppers, Pixies, Singing Mice, Bunny Hoppers, or some mutant strain of all of them mixed together?

The children's record labels greatly resembled their counterparts in the print medium by adding productions starring licensed characters to their Christmas mix. As with the comic books, Little Golden Books, and others, some of these attempts produced more satisfactory results than others.

Little Golden Records had the licensing rights to more different television and cartoon characters than you could shake a cel at, but the company did not use them for many Christmas records, other than a few singles here and there, such as Yogi Bear singing "Have a Hap-Hap-Happy Christmas." Since Daws Butler, the usual voice of Yogi, was contractually tied to another record label, most of his characters on Golden Records were impersonated by radio veteran Gilbert Mack. "Mickey Mouse's Christmas Party," an early 1950s disk that predated the establishment of Disney's own record label, went all out and used the same actors who provided the characters' voices in the cartoons: Jimmy Macdonald as Mickey, Clarence Nash as Donald Duck, and Pinto Colvig as Goofy.

At the same time as the new Grasshoppers series, the identical songs were also issued under the name of the Bunny Hoppers, with references to insects changed to rabbits in the dialogue.

Because Daws Butler, the usual voice of Yogi Bear, was under contract to another company, radio actor Gilbert Mack impersonated Yogi for this Golden Records release.

In 1959, Golden released three Christmas records starring that slapstick team that had recently become a big hit all over again thanks to local children's TV shows, the Three Stooges. The six tunes were also combined onto a single longer-playing release and much, much later were released by nostalgia record label Rhino as an LP. In songs including "Wreck the Halls," "Jingle Bell Drag," and "Down through the Housetop," Moe, Larry, and Curly Joe demonstrate their unique ability to turn Christmas into a federal disaster area. They also enliven such previously established novelty tunes as "All I Want for Christmas Is My Two Front Teeth" and "I Want a Hippopotamus for Christmas," and one even more oddball number, "I Gotta Cold for Christmas":

> Waited by the window sill
> Just for Santa, caught a chill;
> Where's my penicillin pill?
> I gotta cold for Christmas.

Naturally, Disneyland Records did not have to go outside its own studio's stable of stars for Christmas material. The company released soundtrack LPs of two of the Rankin/Bass Christmas specials, *Frosty's Winter Wonderland* and *'Twas the Night before Christmas*, but these were simply the audio portions of the television programs, not original productions especially for records. Then there was the 1975 LP that cast the Disney stars as the characters in Dickens's *A Christmas Carol*. Toward the end of that decade, the company issued an album of standard Christmas songs performed by Larry Groce and a children's choir, but since the cover depicted the well-known Disney characters, some people complained when those beloved figures were nowhere to be heard. The record company responded by having its voice actors come in and add the character voices to the existing recording, allowing Mickey, Goofy, Donald, and the rest to satisfy everyone.

The other animation studio that had its own record company, Hanna-Barbera Records, did not try to capture the Christmas market very heavily. The record division was so busy trying to issue as many LPs featuring the Hanna-Barbera cartoon

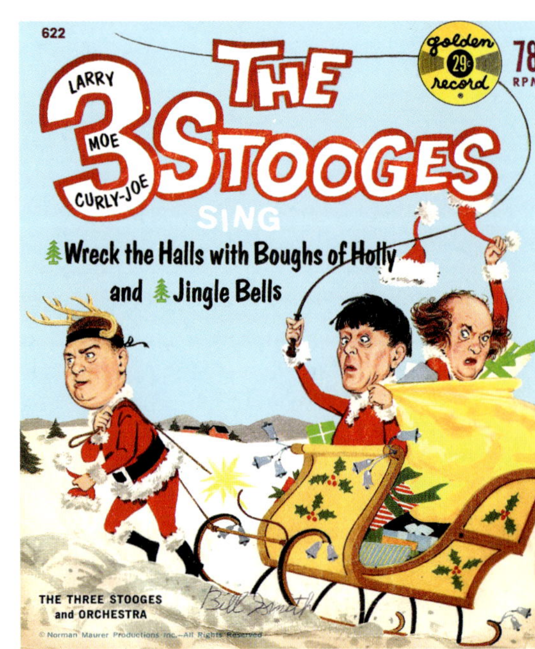

In their 1959 set of Christmas songs, knuckleheads Moe, Larry, and Curly Joe demonstrated their ability to turn a Christmas celebration into a melee of ruin and destruction. BILL SMITH COLLECTION

Left: ***This was one of the Disney Christmas releases that failed to deliver the famous characters depicted on its cover; the songs were rendered by a generic choir, with no characters present.*** **Right:** ***Hanna-Barbera Records also was not above using its beloved characters to sell a product in which they did not appear. The selections on this Christmas LP consisted totally of the "Hanna-Barbera organ and chimes."***

cast as possible, while simultaneously trying to break into the rock-and-roll market with non-cartoon-related singles, that there was not much time left for Christmas cheer. One of its few holiday releases pictured on its cover an orchestra consisting of Yogi Bear, Huckleberry Hound, Snagglepuss, the Flintstones, and other stars playing Christmas selections. As with Disney's Larry Groce LP, imagine how some kids felt when they dropped the needle into the groove and found that not only did the record not feature any of these characters, but it had no vocals at all. The famous old Christmas carols were rendered totally by "the Hanna-Barbera organ and chimes," which obviously had nothing to do with modern Stone Age families or stealing pic-a-nic baskets in Jellystone Park. Heavens to Murgatroyd!

Peter Pan Records enlisted the truly inimitable voice of Mel Blanc for its "Christmas with Bugs Bunny and Friends" LP. Although no copyright date appears on the cover, one piece of internal evidence helps establish an approximate time frame. Bugs and Granny (the one from the Tweety and

Peter Pan Records enlisted the incomparable voice of Mel Blanc for its Bugs Bunny Christmas album; unfortunately, the scripts were not nearly as entertaining as Blanc's bottomless voice box.

Sylvester cartoons, not *The Beverly Hillbillies*) are detained in the western town of Holly by sheriff Yosemite Sam, who suspects them of being the notorious bank robbers Frannie and Slugs. This would seem to indicate that the recording was made around the time of Warner Brothers' hit feature *Bonnie and Clyde* (1968). Certainly Blanc's voice was still in fine form at the time, evidencing none of the coarsening that marked his Peter Pan Records performances of the 1970s. It is still not explained, though, how Yosemite Sam—who was generally portrayed as an outlaw in his cartoons—ended up wearing a badge.

The other three stories on the Bugs LP are relatively timeless. In one of them, Bugs hears a news report that Rudolph, "the VERY Red-Nosed Reindeer," is sick with the flu, and Santa refuses to make his annual journey without his favorite sidekick. Bugs gathers up Porky Pig and Speedy Gonzales to accompany him to the North Pole to help, and the newscaster is soon reporting that Santa's sleigh appears to be led by a creature with long ears instead of antlers. In another story, Bugs and Daffy Duck give psychiatric treatment to Elmer Fudd, who has an irrational belief that he is Santa Claus. Bugs diagnoses Fudd's mental illness as "Santa Claustrophobia." And finally, Bugs has to convince his disbelieving nephew Junior that there really is a Santa Claus. Each of the four stories on the album contains an original song, making the whole package sound much like an animated Christmas special.

In 1977, Peter Pan Records came up with a whole different set of stories for a Popeye Christmas LP starring Jack Mercer, the longtime gravelly voice of the squinch-eyed sailor. The other actors on the album are uncredited, but they are none of the same people who provided voices in the cartoons. The first story involves Popeye shopping for a "wriskwatchk" as a Christmas gift for Olive Oyl, only to be in the jewelry store at the time of a robbery. The two crooks bind Popeye's hands and feet with rope and toss him into the backseat of his own car. Luckily for the plot, the backseat is where Olive has stashed her gift to Popeye: a dozen spinach pies. After devouring all that green stuff, Popeye snaps his bonds like thread and fixes the two jewel thieves good and proper.

In another story, Swee' Pea and some other kids go wailing to Popeye that they wanted to buy a Christmas tree for the poor children of the neighborhood, but the local nursery is owned by the "old meanie" Ebesneezer Stooge, who refuses to sell them his finest tree. His comment on the whole situation: "Hah! Bumbug!" Popeye dresses up as Stooge's deceased business partner, Barley, and scares the Christmas spirit into Stooge, who does not say "Nyuk nyuk nyuk" about it all. In a third, Popeye is playing Santa at a department store when that big bully Bluto has to show up and expose him as a fraud. "There ain't no Santy Claus!" the bearded brute tells the shocked kids. Before Popeye can administer his traditional thrashing, the real Santa shows up and demonstrates that he has his own ways of dealing with bad guys, and it doesn't involve eating spinach. Roaring, "Now feel the power of the great north wind," Santa inflates himself like a balloon and blows subzero air onto Bluto, freezing the old villain's black beard and turning him blue.

In one segment of the Popeye LP from Peter Pan Records, Santa Claus proves that he can handle big bully Bluto without having to resort to eating spinach.

A less ambitious Peter Pan offering was "Bozo's Big Top Christmas Singalong" (1973), with most of the voices provided by Bozo's legal owner, Larry Harmon. Not only did Peter Pan skimp on the budget for actors, but the only musical accompaniment is an organ. Between traditional Christmas songs, there are brief vignettes involving the Bozo cast of characters, which would have been familiar to anyone who watched the Harmon-produced cartoons: Butchy Boy and Belinda, Wacko Wolf, gangsters Big Shorty and Short Biggy, Professor Tweetyfoofer, and "Slippery By, international spy," who initially attempts to make off with the star from the top of the circus Christmas tree. (Quick! Call out the Cinnamon Bear!)

Peter Pan Records even tried coming up with Christmas stories that were not intended to be humorous, as with its trilogy of tales starring DC Comics superheroes Batman, Superman, and Wonder Woman. Comic book fans generally look down their noses at these low-budget productions with cheesy sound effects. In one, Superman defeats a villain who has hidden a nuclear missile inside the national Christmas tree in Washington, D.C., and rigged up a series of others around the country so that when the president pushes the button to light the tree, he will blow up the world. (Pieces on earth, anyone?) Meanwhile, Batman contends with evil carolers, and Wonder Woman is faced with having to rescue Santa Claus from the kidnapping clutches of the German goddess Brunhilde. The three sordid stories were released on an LP and also shortened for a series of separate 45s.

Santa Claus was comin' to clown in George Peed's breathtaking artwork for Peter Pan Records' "Bozo's Christmas Sing-Along."

There might have been a more unlikely pairing of characters than Wonder Woman and Santa Claus, but you might have to think a while to come up with one.

Frequently the covers, or paper sleeves, of all of these records were as memorable as the material contained on the actual disks. Examples of these covers have appeared throughout this chapter, but there is one particular artist whose name has become familiar to generations of former children: George Peed. Because of his distinctive style and the fact that he usually signed his artwork very prominently, Peed's name remains closely associated with the covers he created for Peter Pan Records during the 1960s and early 1970s—not only Christmas records, but many others in that company's catalog as well. Peed's unique style can be identified even in the rare instances that his signature was not included. His drawings were always extremely animated—one can almost see them move

George Peed used his unique style in these two classic Peter Pan Records covers. His artwork was featured on most of the company's releases, both at Christmas and during the rest of the year, from the 1960s into the early 1970s.

just by staring at them—and colorful in the extreme.

It is an established fact that George Peed's artistic reputation usually took a backseat to that of his brother Bill. Bill who, you say? That depends on the period of time you mean. Both brothers worked for the Walt Disney Studios during the 1940s, with Bill receiving screen credit for his contributions as a story artist. In the middle of that decade, Bill's name appeared onscreen as Bill Peed, but by the 1950s he

Above: *This* Rudolph the Red-Nosed Reindeer *punch-out book was another example of Peed's immediately identifiable style of art.* Right: *One of Peed's finest Christmas images for Peter Pan Records was this depiction of Frosty the Snowman standing vigil on a snowy Christmas Eve.*

Unfortunately, sometimes Peed's style did not quite fit the subject matter of the record. Who knew that metal drums and Santa hats were standard equipment at the time the wise men presented their gifts to the baby Jesus?

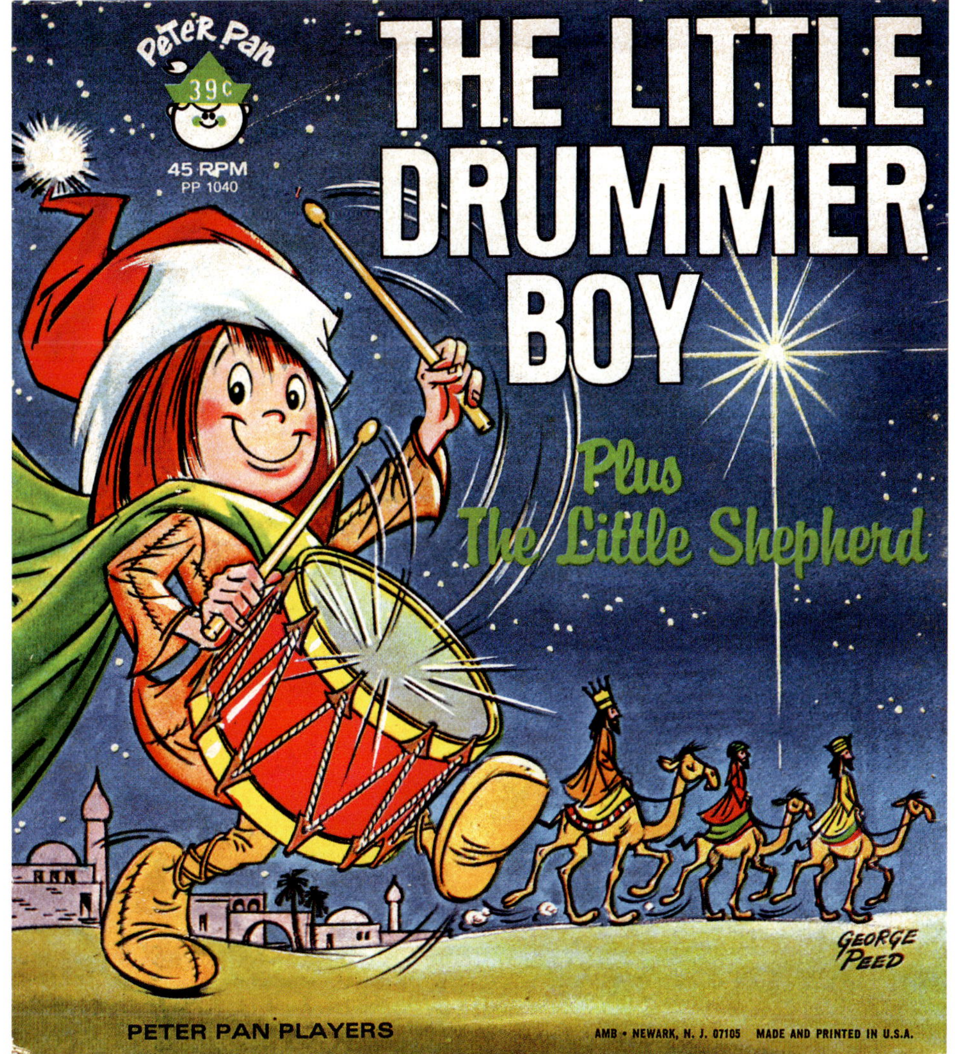

had altered the spelling to Bill Peet, and under that name, he went on to enjoy a successful career as author and illustrator of children's books. (The circumstances surrounding the changing of his name have never been documented, but it is possible to think of at least some reasons why he may have done so.) Brother George had been around since the days of *Fantasia* (1940) but typically did not receive screen credit for his Disney film work.

George Peed's lasting contribution to Disney history was in the licensing and merchandising division, where he turned out castles-full of artwork for Disney-related toys, games, and books. He apparently started freelancing as an artist in the early 1960s, while his Disney work was still going on, as there is a *Rudolph the Red-Nosed Reindeer* "punch-out book" from Golden Books with his unmistakable work. His Peter Pan Records career seems to have begun around the same time, and it is his covers that most people of a certain age associate with that company.

Peed's record covers were always bright, colorful, and cheerful—whether that was called for or not. The problem came when

George Peed's background as a Disney merchandise artist was never more evident than in his cover for Donald look-alike Irwin the Disco Duck's Christmas LP. Those are some cute chicks boogieing down, though. The voice of Irwin was provided by longtime Hanna-Barbera mainstay Don Messick.

such an approach was not appropriate to the subject at hand. He created some stunningly beautiful images for "Frosty the Snowman" and "Silent Night," just to name a few, but he stumbled a bit when it came time for "The Little Drummer Boy." Peed's cover for that classic tune depicts the title character marching merrily behind the camels of the three wise men, beating a red metal drum with all his might, while wearing a goofy grin and a Santa Claus hat atop his head. One could probably think of several things wrong with this whole concept.

Because Peter Pan Records had so many licensed cartoon characters in its lineup, Peed often found himself required to depict familiar figures from many studios other than his alma mater Disney. To put it charitably, he was more comfortable and successful with some of them than with others. He did a terrific job with Bozo on the Christmas LP, but his depictions of Popeye and the Warner Brothers cartoon crowd were, shall we say, a little "off-model." Nevertheless, the resulting look was so distinctive that many children have fond memories even of some of Peed's less-than-accurate work. Therefore, for his contributions to our collective Christmas consciousness, let us all raise our eggnog and propose a toast to the late Christmas record cover artist extraordinaire. Merry Christmas, George Peed, wherever you are!

Deck Them Halls

AND STUFF LIKE THAT

CHAPTER 5

I don't know about you, but my Christmas memories of all the things discussed so far are inextricably tied to mental images of the decorations of that time period. Sometimes the memories are more general, but other times they are sharply specific. To illustrate, I will use an example that relates to the Christmas records that were just discussed.

Over the years, Peter Pan Records endlessly recycled a tune called "The Little Tin Soldier and the Little Toy Drum." It had been rendered as far back as 1959 by the schizophrenic Grasshoppers/Pixies/Bunny Hoppers aggregation, and it was later rerecorded by a male soloist—probably radio mainstay Jack Arthur—as the B side of Peter Pan's version of the "Parade of the Wooden Soldiers." This was another song that, like "March of the Toys" and "Toyland," was not specifically geared toward Christmas but got more exposure during that time of year than any other. I had that particular record as far back as I can remember, and my family also had among our decorations a lighted plastic toy soldier, about sixteen inches tall, that adorned the front window each year. Yes, I still have it, and you can see it pictured on the next page. To this day, I cannot hear "The Little Tin Soldier and the Little Toy Drum" without my mind wandering back to the times I would listen to that record while staring at the toy soldier decoration. Okay, so it's not the most spectacular memory in history—but it's mine, and that's what counts the most.

Now, it would be quite beyond the scope of this book to repeat the many stories—some true, and some legend—behind the establishment of such decorating traditions as candles, holly, and Christmas trees. The origins of those concepts have been well documented elsewhere; for our purposes, we'll look at how they were adapted and

reinvented for the postwar baby boom era. With that goal in mind, let's begin with that centerpiece of most homes during the holiday season: the tree.

Although most families who decorated for Christmas probably would have agreed that the tree was the most visible symbol of their spirit of peace on earth and goodwill

Christmas village glows with light 2.99

Charming handmade storybook houses create fairy tale atmosphere on mantel, on or under the tree . . . children will delight in using them with train sets too. Each tiny house has hanger and can be used as an unusual tree decoration. Miniature lights glow warmly through windows. 2 extra bulbs incl. Imported. Snow not incl.
48 HT 12382—Castle abt. 5½ in. high, houses 2 to 3¼ in. Ship. wt. 1 lb. 1 oz. Set **2.99**

Replacement bulbs for Christmas village. Package of 30 clear bulbs.
48 HT 12344 LX—Ship. wt. 6 oz. . . . . Package **1.99**

Left: *This is the original lighted toy soldier window decoration that I used to stare at while listening to Peter Pan Records' song "The Little Tin Soldier and the Little Toy Drum." If you haven't figured out yet that I'm a sentimental old coot, you haven't been reading very closely.* Above: *I'd guess that the majority of this book's readers had one of these miniature lighted Christmas villages around the base of the tree at one time or another.*

ARTIFICIAL CHRISTMAS TREE WITH LIGHTS

No. X-6867—Artificial Christmas Tree, branches of which are made on a wire and which can be folded up and put away from year to year. The branches are decorated with red berries at the tip of each branch and are also wired with eight electric Christmas tree lights in imitation candle form; 48 in. high and 27 in. wide at the lowest branch. Made with a red wood box base. The tree is well branched. Price, complete with 8 Mazda tree lights, each packed in separate carton........**$6.75**

No. X-6868—Artificial Christmas Tree, similar to No. X-6867 excepting that it is 68 in. high and 34 in. wide at the lowest branch and contains 16 Mazda Christmas tree lights. Price, complete with 16 Mazda tree lights....**$12.50**

Early artificial Christmas trees looked a bit sparse compared with the more realistic ones available later. The description on the left dates from 1928; the Santa and tree on the right were illustrated in the 1942 Montgomery Ward catalog, showing that things had not changed much in the intervening years.

Few decorations exemplify the 1950s and early 1960s as well as the aluminum Christmas tree and accompanying color wheel to illuminate it.

to men, that spirit could turn into war and contempt when it came to the question of a live versus artificial tree. Live tree supporters vowed that artificial trees represented everything that was wrong with a society that preferred plastic over the genuine article; artificial tree aficionados countered that the demand for live trees was destroying the very resource it was intended to honor, and besides that, the combination of drying branches and hot electric lights was a disaster waiting to happen.

Though it may seem that this argument began in the postwar world, when everything else about life was changing drastically, artificial trees actually had been around for years before then. But it was probably the exploding baby boom, and the resulting increased demand for Christmas trees of all needle types, that brought the controversy into the forefront.

Artificial trees came in many different varieties. Some were meant to closely mimic the look of a live tree; you could even buy aerosol spray cans of stuff that was supposed to make them smell real. Others were considerably more stylized and would never be mistaken for something that once grew in nature. Some of these nonrealistic trees resembled nothing so much as collections of bottle brushes sticking out of a wooden pole; not coincidentally, many of them were manufactured by the same companies that produced such brushes the rest of the year.

But the ultimate in getting away from nature was the aluminum tree. It was introduced in 1950 by one of those same year-round brush companies, and its shiny, totally unrealistic look perfectly fit the mood of the Space Race decade. Electric lights were not recommended for a metallic tree, so a second icon of 1950s–60s Christmas decorating came into being: the rotating color wheel, which would bathe the glittering aluminum branches in a succession of colors. The preferred décor for such a tree was minimal: glass ornaments, all of a single color, with no tinsel (which would have looked rather redundant against the feathery branches) or other accessories necessary.

The aluminum tree created a monster—or, in some people's opinions, *was* a monster. Once people had seen that Christmas trees did not have to be green, it was as if someone had unlocked a horrible secret. White trees were fairly standard, with their suggestion of snowy branches, but accord-

The most popular way of decorating aluminum trees was with ornaments of a single color, with no further embellishment necessary. KYLE WEAVER COLLECTION ing to Christmas historian Karal Ann Marling, by the late 1950s, artificial trees were also available in such nontraditional Christmas colors as pink, purple, blue, and mint green, plus many other pastel shades. Weirder still, people began dipping live trees into various concoctions that would dye their formerly natural branches and needles in these new color schemes. Therefore, instead of artificial trees becoming more realistic, for a number of years the live trees began looking artificial.

This then-and-now controversy spilled over into the mass media's depictions of Christmas. You probably all remember the line in *A Charlie Brown Christmas* (1965),

By the time of A Charlie Brown Christmas _(1965), Linus and good ol' Charlie Brown found themselves facing a veritable forest of artificial trees of all shapes and colors._

when good ol' C. B. decides that the school Christmas pageant needs a tree to keep it down to earth, and the girls immediately enthuse that he is right: "Get a big, shiny, aluminum Christmas tree—maybe painted pink!" That remark was obviously not just a figment of Charles M. Schulz's fertile imagination. In 1962, an episode of Lucille Ball's second TV sitcom, *The Lucy Show*, revolved around the fact that she and her divorcée friend Vivian Bagley (Vivian Vance, a.k.a. Ethel Mertz) have drastically different ideas of what constitutes a true family Christmas. It was one thing for one family to open presents on Christmas Eve and the other on Christmas morning; it was still another for one family to have Christmas dinner at 1 P.M. and the other at 6 P.M.; but when Lucy finds that Viv always has a white tree as opposed to her own green one, it means war. Adding insult to injury, Viv accidentally steps on Lucy's favorite childhood ornament, a ratty-looking Santa Claus on a bicycle. "I guess now you'll have to call him Kris Krinkle," Viv cracks.

With the cultural "back to nature" movement of the late 1960s and into the 1970s, the goofier-looking Christmas trees, both artificial and live, fell out of fashion. In more recent years, some manufacturers have begun offering aluminum trees once again, this time aimed at the nostalgia market, and accordingly, they sell for much higher retail prices than the originals. But while trees were settling into a relatively

So, you think aluminum trees were kooky? Get a load of this television antenna variation from the cover of TV Guide's _Christmas 1955 issue._

orderly pattern, what went onto them, and around them, kept evolving.

It is stating the obvious to point out that electric lights did not become commonplace until the majority of U.S. residences had access to electricity, and in some of the

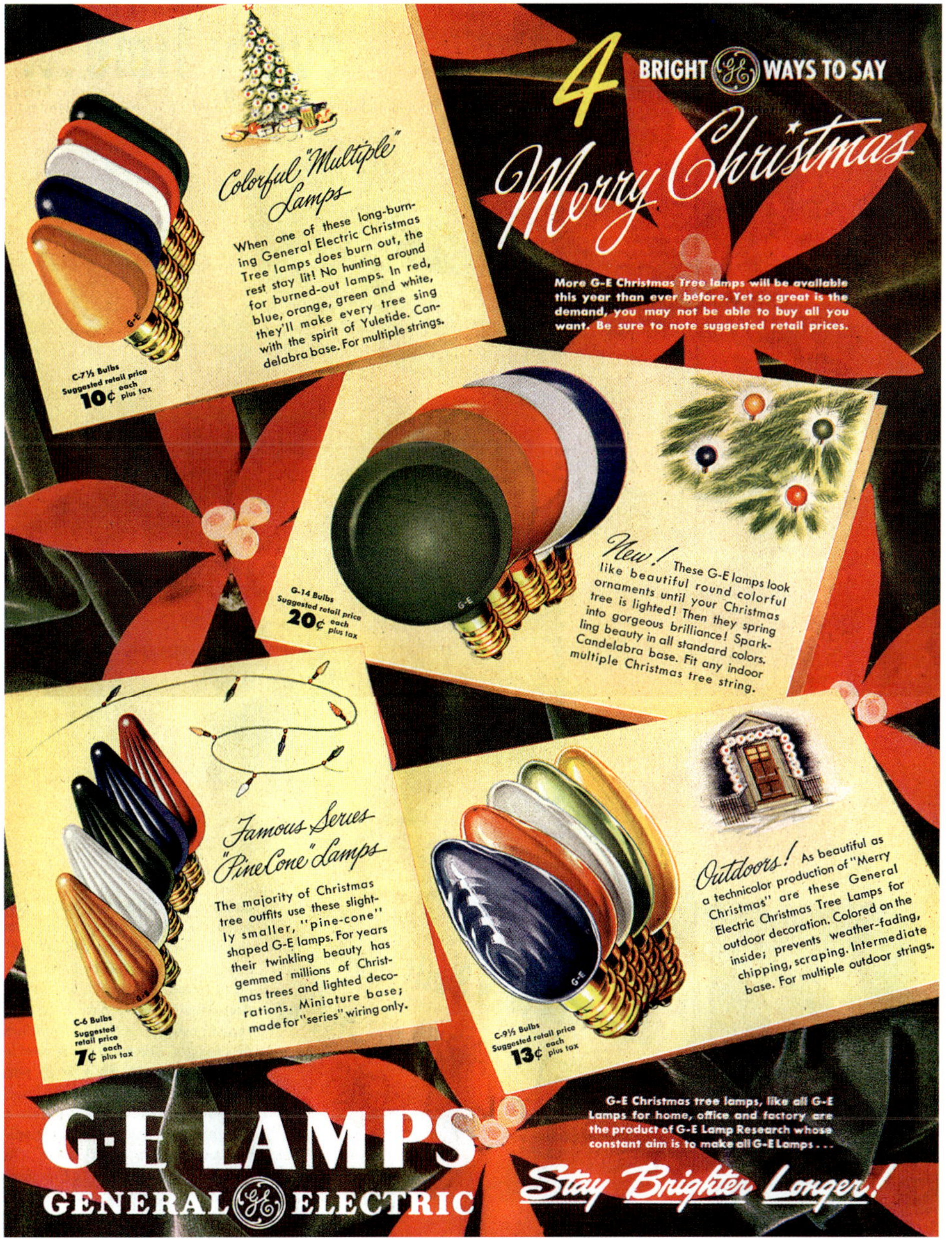

Above: *Electric Christmas lights slowly caught on as more and more parts of the country received electrical service. The boxes were frequently works of art in and of themselves.* **Right:** *This magazine ad illustrated the various types of Christmas lights made by General Electric, from the original pointed C6s to the more familiar C7½s to the flame-shaped outdoor bulbs that were just beginning to become popular.* TODD JONES

4 BRIGHT WAYS TO SAY
Merry Christmas

More G-E Christmas Tree lamps will be available this year than ever before. Yet so great is the demand, you may not be able to buy all you want. Be sure to note suggested retail prices.

Colorful "Multiple" Lamps

When one of these long-burning General Electric Christmas Tree lamps does burn out, the rest stay lit! No hunting around for burned-out lamps. In red, blue, orange, green and white, they'll make every tree sing with the spirit of Yuletide. Candelabra base. For multiple strings.

C-7½ Bulbs
Suggested retail price
10¢ each plus tax

New! These G-E lamps look like beautiful round colorful ornaments until your Christmas tree is lighted! Then they spring into gorgeous brilliance! Sparkling beauty in all standard colors. Candelabra base. Fit any indoor multiple Christmas tree string.

G-14 Bulbs
Suggested retail price
20¢ each plus tax

Famous Series "Pine Cone" Lamps

The majority of Christmas tree outfits use these slightly smaller, "pine-cone" shaped G-E lamps. For years their twinkling beauty has gemmed millions of Christmas trees and lighted decorations. Miniature base; made for "series" wiring only.

C-6 Bulbs
Suggested retail price
7¢ each plus tax

Outdoors! As beautiful as a technicolor production of "Merry Christmas" are these General Electric Christmas Tree Lamps for outdoor decoration. Colored on the inside; prevents weather-fading, chipping, scraping. Intermediate base. For multiple outdoor strings.

C-9½ Bulbs
Suggested retail price
13¢ each plus tax

G-E LAMPS
GENERAL ELECTRIC

G-E Christmas tree lamps, like all G-E Lamps for home, office and factory are the product of G-E Lamp Research whose constant aim is to make all G-E Lamps . . .

Stay Brighter Longer!

more rural areas, that could have been as late as the post-World War II years. While they were undergoing their long process of catching on, by 1920 the bulbs used for Christmas tree lights had evolved into the familiar "pine cone" shape with which most of us are familiar. Originally known as C6s, in 1934 they were joined by C7½s, which still had a pointed tip but were larger and more bulbous at the bottom. C7½s did not really become popular until after the war. Their big selling point was that if one bulb burned out, the rest of the string remained lighted—unlike the C6s, where a burnout meant the whole set went dark. The C7½s came in variations: Most bulbs were a solid color, but others were transparent and usually twinkled, meaning they blinked at irregular intervals.

A 1950 import from Italy known originally as Fairy Lights changed the way people thought of decorating their trees. These mini-lights, as they soon became known familiarly, put out so much less heat and were so much easier to install—simply draping them over the branches, rather than having to painstakingly clip each socket to a supporting twig—that they soon became the most common type of tree lighting. Like aluminum trees, which have not gone away completely, the older-style screw-in bulbs are still around, and many homeowners continue to prefer their glow—intense heat and all.

Miniature lights, first imported from Italy in 1950, became the preferred form of lighting up an artificial tree by the late 1960s.

Another type of light that had a shorter lifespan was the fondly remembered bubble light. Several different manufacturers produced these, especially in the late 1940s and 1950s, and many former kids remember staring at them as an integral part of the Christmas season. That was actually the safest thing to do with them; since their whole appeal was that the heat from the light caused a small vial of liquid, usually methylene chloride, to bubble and boil atop each bulb, one can easily imagine how hot they could become after being lit for a while. Even though methylene chloride has a relatively low boiling point, safety concerns, plus the novelty wearing off, are probably what doomed the bubble lights to the antique stores. Just like the once-reviled aluminum trees, though, some companies have recently begun making bubble lights once again, usually packaged in beautiful reproductions of their original boxes.

One of the major manufacturers of Christmas lights was NOMA (an acronym for National Outfit Manufacturing Association), which produced all of the above types. In a postwar sales brochure, NOMA did about as good a job as anyone ever did in tying its vested business interests to the meaning of the holiday, editorializing:

> With the coming of the Yuletide season, every city, town and hamlet bedecks itself in glowing splendor. Throughout the land, on every hill, in every vale, millions of colorful lights sparkle a friendly welcome. In the enchantment of this magic glow, all grief is shorn and the heart is filled with gladness—for the true spirit of Christmas is naught but the spirit of light. In the quiet darkness of the evening, each tiny gleam is like a beacon which softly lights the way to "Peace on earth, Good Will to men."

And while all of that was certainly true enough, if it happened to increase NOMA's sales of indoor and outdoor lights, so much the merrier.

Although the baby boomer years saw a lot of variety in the types of Christmas tree

This ad from the NOMA corporation, responsible for the majority of Christmas lights available in the 1940s and 1950s, includes the famous bubble lights that so many baby boomers recall watching intently. TODD JONES

lights, this was nothing compared with the many different types of ornaments. Credit for creating the demand for ornaments in the first place is usually given to that pioneer of retail (and Christmas) merchandising, F. W. Woolworth. In the 1880s, Woolworth began importing large quantities of handcrafted glass ornaments from Germany and selling them in his chain of dime stores. Unlike later glass ornaments, which were usually sold in boxed dozens, Woolworth sold his individually. Their beauty soon made obsolete any earlier forms of tree decorations, which tended toward paper and thus were not always compatible with trees lit by candles.

How many of us remember, as kids, looking into the colored balls hanging from the tree branches and making funny faces, which were made even funnier by the distorted images in the curved glass? But the same trends in decorating that affected trees and lights put their own spin on the ornaments too. Joining and sometimes replacing the glass ornaments were the "satin" ornaments, made from balls of Styrofoam covered with tiny silken threads. These were nice when new but usually became a bit nappy-looking as the threads started to unravel. Companies specializing in plastics came out with a whole variety of ornaments that contained miniature scenes, such as Nativity figures or more secular Santas and snowmen, inside. There were even miniature motors that could be attached to the hangers, so that each ornament could slowly rotate and show off all its angles.

A

B

C

D

E

F

Now at Wards—20 miniature lights!
Two 10-light strings at *one* low price!

Wards special convenience package of 2 strings of 10 lights each includes 4 extra bulbs; add-on plugs so strings may be connected. Lightweight green cord won't pull branches down. Push-in type bulbs—if one goes out, the others remain lighted. Recommended for indoor use on all non-metallic trees and displays.

Above: ***By far the most popular glass ornaments were the ones made under the Shiny Brite label. Even straight shooter Roy Rogers used them to decorate his tree on the cover of this 1953 comic book.*** DONNIE PITCHFORD **Left:** ***By the late 1960s, miniature lights were the most common and could be purchased with a mind-boggling variety of coverings to break up the monotony of the bare bulbs.***

Supplementing the lights and ornaments were various kinds of garlands and tinsel. Strands of plastic candy and popcorn were available for those who did not have the time, or interest, to make the real thing. The traditional fuzzy tinsel garland was, for a time, the most common adornment, but there were occasional forays into new realms. Some people used what were called rope garlands, which resembled pieces of aluminum foil twisted together to form narrow, stringlike trim. Others liked the angel hair made from spun glass, but perhaps most popular of all were the long, shiny, silver strands of tinsel known as icicles. A lot of patience was required to apply these to a tree properly; when done well, the tree shimmered as if recently exposed to an ice storm, but those who rushed the job would wind up with the supposed icicles looking more like tangled globs clinging to the branches. Many such decorations were lead-based and could have toxic effects if eaten, as young children often tried to do. That danger was realized fairly early on, and some manufacturers, including the ubiquitous Doubl-Glo brand, made it a point to specify "lead-free" on their packaging.

Just as the old-fashioned Christmas bulbs had made way for the minilights, so did breakable glass ornaments step aside for more durable varieties, including these "satin" ornaments, which unfortunately tended to unravel after a few uses.

New . . . unusual! Lighted ornaments for enchantment

$4, $6 Set of 10

[1] [2] New idea combines lights and ornaments to trim your tree or mantel, around windows, doors more effectively than ever before. Whimsically gay and dramatically beautiful—10 three dimensional Christmas scenes glitter under miniature lights. Two extra bulbs incl. Other lights, pg. 184, 185.

(1) **Deluxe set—ten 5-in.** ornament lights. Made in Italy—exquisitely detailed scenes typical of the Old World artisan. For extra bulbs, order 48 HT 12341LX, page 185.
48 HT 12358—Ship. wt. 1 lb. 13 oz. . . . .Set **6.00**

(2) **Set of ten 2¾-in.** ornament lights. For extra bulbs, order 48 HT 12345LX, pg. 185.
48 HT 12390—Ship. wt. 13 oz. . . . . .Set **4.00**

Satin balls 6.99 Set of 12

Old favorites—unbreakable 3¼-in. balls richly hand decorated in Old World elegance. Perfect for coordinated decorating of tree, suspend in windows, heap in bowl for a centerpiece. Cheaper by the dozen at Wards so you achieve THE look for less. Ship. wt. 1 lb. 12 oz.
48 HT 12181 L. . . . . .Set **6.99**

Drums 5.88 Set of 12

To delight any child, decorate your tree or gift packages with this big, low-cost set of 12 miniature drums. Each fashioned by hand—lightweight, unbreakable—about 3 in. high. Each with cord for hanging on tree at playing angle. Ship. wt. 1 lb. 8 oz. Order now and Charge It!
48 HT 12177 L. . . . . .Set **5.88**

A Wards exclusive 3.88 Set of 8

New collection of winsome figures set into colorful balls to give each full dimensional effect—angels, snowmen and gift-bearing elves. You won't find them anywhere else—they were imaginatively crafted exclusively for Wards in pressed composition—colorful, 3⅛-in. ornaments for your tree—or suspend on ribbons in your windows.
48 HT 12175 L—Wt. 1 lb. 3 oz. . .Set **3.88**

Traditional collection 2.99 Set of 12

Delicately handcrafted glass ornaments imported from W. Germany where craftsmen have perfected this centuries-old art. Exquisitely detailed, artistically colored. Each of the 12 is different—Father Christmas, a bird, a bell, pitcher, horn, balls and drops with mirror-like finishes, decorated with glitter or frosting. About 2½ to 5¾ in. high. Ship. wt. set of 12, 2 lbs. 6 oz.
48 HT 12190—Set. . . .**2.99** 2 sets. **5.79**

Frolicking Santas 2.53 Set of 12

Santa himself in three different animated poses, will decorate your tree or packages, peer out of the top of a stuffed stocking. Twelve 4-in. figures complete in every detail from furry trim to fluffy beard.
48 HT 12176 L—Ship. wt. 11 oz. . . . . .Set **2.53**

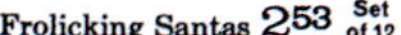

182 WARDS ALL **Charge It, see page 348**

Snow scenes 2.99 Set of 12

Just shake to create a flurry of snowflakes! Six different 3 dimensional scenes in molded plastic. 2½ in. high. Wonderful paper weights, mantel or table decoration, or for stockings.
48 HT 12687 L—Ship. wt. 3 lbs. 8 oz. . . . . . . .Set **2.99**

Christmas trees, pg. 186; lights, pgs. 184, 185.

48 miniature toys . . . 1.99 Set
Ideal stocking stuffers

Plenty for all, big family or small . . . pipes, whistles, cars, boats, purses, carts, (stocking not included). For Christmas or birthday party favors. 48 pcs. in set—all plastic.
48 HT 12599—Ship. wt. 10 oz. . . . . . .Set 1.99

Above: *How many of you remember your dad yelling in frustration after trying to get the stringy silver icicles to hang properly from the tree branches or getting irritated skin from the spun-glass angel hair?* Left: *By 1967, Montgomery Ward was offering ornaments that resembled nearly everything* except *traditional tree decorations.*

The tree was the focal point of most homes, but there were other ways to deck the halls . . . and living room and bathroom and kitchen. For modern suburban dwellings that did not come with the nostalgia of built-in fireplaces, cardboard replicas were available to provide the suitable hearthside touch. The fake fireplace made a handy place to hang stockings and provided a mantel to decorate, and it usually even came with a bulb and tinfoil reflector to give the impression of a flickering fire. But unlike the real thing, rather than having to keep it clean, when Christmas was over, it could be folded flat into its storage carton and packed away in the attic or garage for the next eleven months.

Even more popular than cardboard fireplaces were the candoliers, or plastic artificial candles, that could be seen in windows across the nation. These were made by many different companies and came in just as many different configurations. Single candles were always popular, but candoliers also came in groups of three and five, as well as the king-size eight-candle version. Candoliers were first made during the era of the pointed C6 bulbs, but they were later adapted for C7½s and continue to sell today. More often than not, they came packaged with their own orange bulbs, the better to simulate candle flames, but once installed in windows, they could be found glowing with any other color available: blue, green, or red flames, or for some true nonconformists, a different color flame in each candle. The only rule for decorating the home was that there were no rules, and that was a large part of the fun.

Those who did not have a real fireplace for Santa to make his grand entrance could get by with this cardboard replica, which could be folded up and stored away until next Christmas.

Once the inside of the house had gone berserk with decorations, it was time to see what could be done about the exterior. Since most suburban dwellings had garages

Above: ***Candoliers for a home's windows came in many different configurations, with the five- and eight-light varieties being the largest and most elaborate. Somehow, over the years, NOMA managed to change the dominant colors of the box from red and green to red and . . . puce?*** **Right:** ***These oversize posters were sold as garage door decorations, once the suburbs proved to be the habitat of choice in the postwar period.***

attached, there were even ways to make these portals into a Christmas greeting. The infamous Spencer catalog offered garage door coverings that could be personalized with the family name. Other companies made oversize posters depicting Santa's grinning face or, for a more reverent look, the wise men atop their camels, following the star of Bethlehem. Now it's personal memory time: One homeowner in our town had the Santa face version, but since his garage did not face the street, he used it in a different way. The brick front of his split-level house had a huge blank space between the windows of the upper and lower floors, so this creative soul mounted the Santa face directly onto the brick wall, with a floodlight shining up from the lawn below. It looked like a giant Christmas billboard. Another townsman had the wise men version and used it in its proper place, on the garage door. Both of these became much-anticipated sights each holiday season, when my parents would take me out to see the neighborhood decorations.

Countless other former kids remember the excitement of riding around their neighborhoods with their parents on cold December nights to see the various displays. This

Once outdoor decorating became a fad, some people took the concept to considerable extremes of taste. The neighbors either enjoyed it or muttered under their breath at all the cars stopping so folks could gawk at the sight.

For the most part, outdoor lights remained outdoors—either on the shrubbery or around the eaves of the house. This homeowner, however, elected to use outdoor C9 bulbs on the live tree in the living room.
TIM CAVENDER

tradition continues to this day, although in this era of mass marketing and ubiquitous retailers such as Walmart, it is far more likely that today's decorated houses and lawns will look a whole lot alike, with many of the same decorations appearing over and over again. During the period this book covers, outdoor decorating tended to be considerably more individualized.

Strings of Christmas lights manufactured specifically for outdoor use had been marketed since 1927. Originally, decorating an area of any size with them would have been quite a chore—not to mention expensive—because each set had only seven lights. Karal Ann Marling reports that General Electric began pushing outdoor Christmas lights heavily in 1947, and their use in outlining the roofs of houses and illuminating lawn shrubbery soon snowballed to fall right in with the wacko goings-on inside with the multicolored trees. This was another custom that ended up being spoofed in *A Charlie Brown Christmas*, with Chuck dismayed to learn that his own dog has won first prize in a neighborhood decoration contest—considered the ultimate sign of vulgar commercialism.

By 1960 or thereabouts, people had decided that lights were not enough; they wanted illuminated representations of all the different familiar Christmas symbols, and a collection of just a few or many of these could become a status symbol of sorts. One lawn decoration that has remained popular over the years is Santa Claus with his sleigh and reindeer. Some of the first such setups marketed for home use involved more than a little of the do-it-yourself mentality so prevalent in the 1950s. Outlets such as hardware stores sold sheets of vinyl preprinted with remarkably lifelike and detailed artwork depicting jolly old St. Nick and his flying quadrupeds. Would-be exterior decorators were required to mount these shapes on a wooden backing, and then painstakingly cut them out. When done well and illuminated with floodlights, such a scene could be most memorable. Many other Christmas staples were also produced in this manner, including angelic carolers and Nativity scenes (which were also marketed already mounted on backings, saving a lot of work). Some companies still sell preprinted vinyl reindeer for dedicated do-it-yourselfers, but the results are not seen on lawns nearly as often as they once were.

The next leg of Santa's journey from legend to lawn took the form of flat sleigh-and-deer sets made of plastic. These were infinitely smaller than the preprinted vinyl variety—the deer stood less than 2 feet tall—and were illuminated by "footlights," white bulbs at the feet of each deer and the runners of the sleigh, with aluminum foil reflectors that were supposed to direct the light upward. From more than 10 feet away, however, this style of scene looked like nothing but a row of white lights.

Sears was marketing these "flat deer" sets in its catalog at least as early as 1962, but many more of them were sold through the legendary Spencer Gifts catalogs later in the decade. While Sears had the decency to describe these sets accurately, the copywriters at Spencer should have had noses that resembled Pinocchio's by the time they got through concocting their hype.

Top: ***This was one of the first Santa-and-reindeer sets produced as lawn decorations, printed on vinyl that had to be mounted on plywood and then cut out with a saw.*** **Bottom:** ***This variation on the "flat deer" idea was available in the early 1960s, but in the late 1970s, Sears brought it back for a brief, unsuccessful encore.***

At the same time the do-it-yourself "flat deer" were prancing across lawns, hark! . . . a similar-style Nativity scene was also heralding its arrival.

Spencer blatantly described the sleigh and deer as "all lit up in 3-dimension," and otherwise indicated that the whole outfit would make a traffic-stopping display on any front lawn. That might have been true, had they elaborated that the only way for people to get a decent view of such a setup would be to stop their cars, get out, and walk across the lawn until they were directly in front of it.

Somewhere amid the emergence of the vinyl deer and flat plastic varieties was another type of decoration that proved to be less durable, both physically and culturally. An almost forgotten style was composed of two bas-relief halves that were attached together to form a single figure, usually with some sort of illumination inside. While the nighttime effect could be quite satisfactory, the inherently fragile nature of such figures doomed them to the Christmas netherworld once something more stable came along.

Around 1962, a new manufacturing process known as blow-molding was introduced, which produced fully rounded figures that not only could stand on their own, but also were illuminated from within. Several companies began blowing out blowmolds as fast as their molds could multiply, and in 1966 came what was apparently the first attempt at bringing Santa and his antlered friends to a statuary form of life.

The original blow-molded sleigh-and-deer design harked back to what had been done before, in that the reindeer figures were not lighted and required a floodlight to illuminate them. On the plus side, they did actually appear in 3-D (Spencer Gifts' earlier claims notwithstanding). The pair of white deer came with a rather simplified

Spencer Gifts plumbed new depths of deceptive advertising in its catalog descriptions of the tiny, flat plastic reindeer the company sold for years. Notice that the small illustration hints that the display could be turned to face any direction—a difficult thing to do when the pieces were printed on only one side.

sleigh holding a Santa figure that contained an interior lightbulb.

Let me now introduce a company that would have much influence on Christmas decorations for a decade. The Poloron Corporation of New Rochelle, New York, had its icy fingers in a number of different products, including insulated jugs and ice coolers, among others. In 1964, Poloron began adding outdoor decorations to its product line; in 1967, the company introduced a new and improved model of the reindeer team. Now the sleigh and deer were illuminated from within—60-watt bulbs in both the sleigh and Santa's body and two 7-watt bulbs in each orange-colored deer—and the scene really could take on an impressive scale. Some people chose to stick with the two deer that came as standard equipment, but others splurged and acquired the proper number of eight.

Did I say the proper number was eight? Well, that's what people had been thinking since at least the 1820s—but then that blinking-beaked troublemaker Rudolph came along and upset the whole even-numbered balance. A quick survey of earlier lawn decorations seems to indicate that despite Rudolph's popularity in story, comic books, and song, little thought was given to making him an official part of home decorating until

Above: ***Even though these 1966 reindeer were 3-D, made through the new blow-molding process, they still required a floodlight to illuminate them.*** **Left:** ***Some homeowners got around the copyright infringement issue by creating their own Rudolphs; this one used a standard plastic lawn deer with a red bulb attached to its nose.***

the 1964 debut of Rankin/Bass's groundbreaking animated special. Suddenly, if a reindeer display did *not* include Rudolph's famed headlight leading the way, kids of all ages, in all parts of the country, would demand—loudly—to know why he was not there.

This posed somewhat of a dilemma for the decoration manufacturers. No one owned exclusive rights to Santa and the other eight beasts of burden, but Rudolph was a copyrighted property, and a company would be required to pay a hefty sum in licensing fees if it was to produce effigies of him for public consumption. Faced with the lack of "real" Rudolphs, many enterprising lawn decorators created their own lead deer by wiring a red lightbulb into an otherwise-standard Poloron deer's nose area. The Garrison-Wagner Company of St. Louis sold a set of reindeer that looked nothing like the Poloron model, and this company skirted the dangerous precipice of trademark infringement by selling a ninth deer billed as Red-Nose Rudy. Those who owned the older vinyl-on-plywood deer also added Robert May's little gold mine to their displays by means of a judiciously attached socket and bulb. In all of Rudolph's many unofficial lawn and rooftop appearances, the lighted nose was the one consistent thing—although even it showed some variety, as some people chose to have it burning steadily, whereas others preferred to hook the socket to a blinker.

The deer were not the first, and far from the only, Christmas figures produced by Poloron. The company's wares first showed up in the 1964 Sears Christmas catalog, in the form of a short and squat snowman.

JUNIOR SIZE DEER TEAM

38 in. high reindeer made of weatherproof vinyl with interior illumination for spectacular night-time attraction. Available in teams of eight and in starter sets of four, with and without Santas. Red-Nose Rudy (with lit-up nose) is available also. When ordering, specify stock number desired.

No. 37-5-38—Complete set with eight deer, one Rudy, one #16 sleigh and one Standing Santa. Specify ground stand or aerial harness. Per set.......... **$289.50**

No. 37-4-38—Complete set with eight deer, one Rudy, one #16 sleigh and one Half Santa. Specify ground stand or aerial harness. Per set.......... **$269.50**

Christmas Profits Begin with POLORON

GIANT SIZE ILLUMINATED DECORATIONS

- HI-IMPACT
- WEATHERPROOF
- TRANSLUCENT
- UNBREAKABLE PLASTIC

Merry Christmas

No. C84-1 GIANT ILLUMINATED SNOWMAN. Holding Detachable Shovel. Stands 48″ high, full, round. Colorfully decorated in vivid Christmas colors. Made of unbreakable weatherproof plastic. Base can be ballasted with sand or gravel. Supplied with U. L. listed cord and socket (no bulb). Packed in poly bag—one per carton.

No. C91-1 ILLUMINATED STANDING SNOWMAN. Holding Detachable Broom. Stands 32″ high. Full, Round. White. with red and black decoration and realistic broom. Made of unbreakable plastic. Base can be ballasted with sand or gravel. U. L. listed cord and single socket (no bulb). Packed in poly bag—one per carton.

UL

Above: ***In 1965, the Garrison-Wagner company sold all eight reindeer plus a mysterious ninth one with a glowing proboscis, identified as Red Nose Rudy.*** **Right:** ***Poloron's first blow-molded snowman design was the small one at right, which actually resembled a dog more than a person. The giant 4-foot model (left) remained a popular item for many years.*** MEL FISCHER

When I was a child (you can insert your own smart-aleck remark here about how I haven't grown up since), only one house in the neighborhood had one of these original Poloron snowmen. Remember, in those days, not every house had the same thing, as they often do today. (Coincidentally, this was the same homeowner who had the wise men cover on his garage door.) The snowman's large, black nose and red earmuffs protruding from underneath his hat made me think he was supposed to be a dog instead of a humanoid snow figure. Check the photo on page 135 and judge for yourself, Rover.

Poloron improved its quality over the years, and by the early 1970s, the company had enough different figures to fill an entire page of the Sears catalog by itself. The company struck Christmas gold with its king-size, 4-foot-tall Santa and snowman figures. Santa was the more commonly seen of the two, holding a present in one hand and putting his finger to his lips with the other, in a "shushing" pose. The snowman could have passed for Frosty, except that Poloron did not pay royalties to Hill and Range Music any more than to Robert May. Poloron's snowman had the traditional black top hat, but instead of a broomstick, he held a molded Christmas wreath in his right hand and a red plastic shovel with "Merry Christmas" in white lettering in his left. Poloron also produced a line of 4-foot-tall carolers that today command outrageous prices on eBay, probably because fewer people bought them than Santas and snowmen. The com-

By 1969, the Poloron line of outdoor decorations had reached incredible heights. The illuminated sleigh and reindeer made one of the most impressive displays the company offered.

pany got really carried away in the late 1960s and made 5-foot-tall Santa and snowman figures that contained interior motors to make them swing back and forth at the waist. The rotating Santa held aloft a lighted lantern, while the snowman grasped a shovel as if he were trying to clear a path. Their size and cost, added to the inherent problems with keeping their motors in operating order, gave these animated greeters a relatively short life in stores.

Not forgetting the real meaning of Christmas, Poloron marketed two different sizes of illuminated Nativity scenes. The larger one, naturally, had the most detailed figures, with the majority of effort expended on the three wise men. Poloron's rendition of this famous trio followed legend and folklore more than what little information St. Matthew gave about them in the Bible, depicting one as an elderly Caucasian, one as a middle-aged Asian, and the third as a young African. Each was decorated with numerous plastic jewels that sparkled in daylight, when the figures' interior illumination could not be seen. It would have been difficult to go far astray in the design of the rest of the tableaux, although discriminating critics might have pointed out that in real life, Mary and the baby

The cover of Poloron's catalog depicted its mechanized Santa, which rotated at the waist, swinging a lighted "Noel" lantern.
MEL FISCHER

Jesus were unlikely to have had the blond hair Poloron assigned to them.

Poloron's entire Christmas line, secular and sacred alike, was decimated in 1973, when then-president Richard Nixon strongly suggested that people stop decorating their yards in order to cut down on energy usage. Since each Poloron figure generally used a 60- or 75-watt bulb, and some figures required two of them, the company found it impossible to survive this decree from on high. The various pieces were gradually discontinued, with the Nativity scenes hanging on until 1977 or somewhere thereabouts. In the years since Poloron's downfall, various other companies have purchased the molds and produced their own cheaper versions for mass consumption. The 4-foot Poloron snowman turned up in this form a few years back, and versions of the smaller Nativity set can still be found at Walmart to this day. For the most part, the new figures lack the color detailing of the originals, and most certainly are made of a thinner, less weather-resistant grade of plastic.

Poloron's most enthusiastic competitor was Empire Plastics of North Carolina, a conglomerate that was also involved in the manufacturing of toys and many other synthetic products. Empire's Christmas line included an extensive number of small figures intended for indoor use but often featured large versions of the same ones for the lawn. The toy soldier that figured in the story that started off this chapter was one of these that existed in both forms. Empire had its own 4-foot snowman holding a wreath and candy cane (and a small indoor version of the same type), plus another snowman bedecked in a blue tailcoat and red derby. Snowmen must have made Empire positively giddy, because yet another design marketed briefly was a snowman dressed as an Emmett Kelly-type tramp clown. For a while, both the Poloron and Empire figures were painted using fluorescent Day-Glo colors, which looked great when new but did not hold up well after years of weathering. Empire managed to keep going for several years after Poloron bit the snowbank, but it too eventually succumbed to higher energy costs.

A number of other companies also made outdoor decorations, but none to the extent of Poloron and Empire. A company called Beco had its own line of carolers and deer as far back as 1962, but as with the early Poloron figures, some were lighted from the inside and others were not. Beco's original carolers, for example, did not have interior illumination but merely bulbs concealed in their hymnals to cast light on their angelic faces.

This was the larger of at least two different Nativity scenes offered by Poloron from the late 1960s well into the 1970s.

Elaborate and electricity-draining decorating like this received a crippling blow in 1973, when President Nixon requested that people cease such extravagant displays in order to battle the perceived energy crisis.

In recent years, various companies have produced new lines of outdoor figures—even including a series of licensed Disney characters—but since these are sold through many more retail outlets than Poloron or Empire ever had available, that also means they are far more common sights along our neighborhood streets of today. While Sears was so heavily involved with its Winnie the Pooh franchise, the chain marketed through its catalog a very large illuminated Pooh wearing a Santa hat and carrying a pot of his beloved "hunny." Even with Sears's mass merchandising muscle, these Poohs are relatively scarce today; more often seen are the smaller Poohs (and an accompanying Tigger) that were available at Walmart.

You have probably realized, without being told, that the type of outdoor decorating described above has now largely been replaced with the ever-popular figures that are simply outlined in lights rather than being 3-D statues. Large Christmas shops can provide these in a seemingly infinite variety

For a period of time, both Poloron and Empire painted their figures in fluorescent Day-Glo colors. Empire sold this small snowman as a window decoration, but also made a 4-foot version for lawn use.

of shapes and styles, and many of them make use of the same animation technology that enabled the fondly remembered neon signs of our youth to operate—multiple arms that light in stages to make Santa Claus wave, and so forth. Running mitten-in-mitten with these is the recent craze for inflatable lawn decorations, which are strongly reminiscent of the balloons in the Macy's Thanksgiving Day Parade. Licensing has played a bigger role in these "airblown" inflatables than in any previous form of outdoor decorating, with figures representing Charlie Brown and his crowd, the Rankin/Bass characters, and the Grinch, among many others.

Will these be the fond childhood memories of today's kids forty years from now? Maybe so, but one way to ensure that is to bundle up your spouse and young'uns and head out into the neighborhoods to see them. Stick a CD of Christmas music in your car's player while you do so, and encourage everyone to sing along—but for the love of Frosty, please forget about text messaging for one evening, and leave the cell phones at home!

CITY SIDEWALKS, Busy Sidewalks

CHAPTER 6

For more decades than anyone can count by this time, each generation has moaned that its Christmas celebrations have become "too commercial." Well, as Mark Twain once famously said about the weather, everyone talks about it, but no one does anything about it. Perhaps that is because, as loath as most people would be to admit it, it is the commercial aspects of Christmas that created some of our fondest memories. Certainly there are millions for whom the real meaning of Christmas is front and center, but that always has pertained, and always will, more to how December 25 is observed. The weeks leading up to the big day belonged to anticipation, and no one was better at building anticipation than the businesses that depended on holiday sales to get them through the rest of the year.

We have already seen how such retail kingpins as Montgomery Ward were responsible for creating future Christmas icons such as Rudolph (and his dimmer brethren, Uncle Mistletoe, Mr. Bingle, and the rest), but it was the arrival of their much-anticipated Christmas mail-order catalogs shortly after Labor Day each year that truly proved the holiday season was not far off. When most people think of Christmas catalogs, they think of the masterpieces published by Sears, Roebuck and Company (although many other companies had their own catalogs that were virtually indistinguishable from Sears's). As hard as it may be to believe, Sears managed to get along just fine for nearly half a century before beginning an annual Christmas catalog. The company was founded in 1886 and issued its first catalog in 1888, but until 1933, any Christmas merchandise was simply lumped in with the last catalog of the year. As if that were not enough of a surprise for you, consider this fact: It was

Left: ***Even before the term "Wish Book" was registered as a trademark, to many people that name was inseparable from giant retailer Sears, Roebuck and Company.*** POLLY CHAMBERS **Right:** ***The 1942 Montgomery Ward Christmas catalog included items that soon became unavailable as a result of the ongoing war, such as metal toys and many types of candy.***

1968 before the Sears Christmas catalog was officially known as the Wish Book.

As far back as the Depression days—and maybe even longer than that—the term "wish book" had been used to describe any mail-order catalog, from any store. The phrase was particularly common in rural communities, where catalogs were the only window into the shopping world that lay beyond the neighborhood general store. Someone at Sears must have remembered hearing the term and had the bright idea of applying it to the Christmas catalog, because within a few years, the formerly generic name had been registered as a Sears trademark, and it remains so today. Sears stopped publishing catalogs regularly in 1993; they since have been eclipsed by the Internet. On the occasions when the company has temporarily revived the Christmas catalog, it still carries the Wish Book title—no doubt a requirement for keeping the trademark from lapsing.

Much obvious care and attention were lavished on the Sears Christmas catalog, both as the Wish Book and in its earlier incarnations. The covers were frequently works of photographic art, although at times paintings were used instead. The position of the all-important toy section was shifted from year to year; sometimes it was the first thing encountered upon opening the front cover, and other times it was saved for the end of the catalog. Frequently the first few pages were devoted to extraspecial merchandise that the company wanted to highlight separately from the departments where it would normally have appeared. In 1967, there was a big push on Disney's Snow White and the Seven Dwarfs merchandise, to tie in with the animated movie's rerelease in theaters and its simultaneous thirtieth anniversary, and Sears proved it was not grumpy, but happy, by devoting several pages to the colorful clutter. It was just what the Doc ordered.

Beginning with the 1965 catalog, Sears was inextricably yoked with another Disney property, that willy nilly silly old bear Winnie the Pooh. As part of the campaign to prepare audiences for Disney's first Pooh cartoon, released in February 1966, Sears signed up as the distributor of a whole exclusive line of merchandise—not only toys, but also the well-remembered Winnie the Pooh brand of children's clothing. The bear

This line of merchandise was heavily promoted to tie in with the thirtieth anniversary of Disney's animated feature* Snow White and the Seven Dwarfs *in 1967.

became a big part of the Christmas catalog, naturally. The 1972 catalog even featured the teddy bear and his equally plush friends on the cover, and the opening pages were devoted to a series of illustrated vignettes in which the denizens of the Hundred Acre Wood acted out various Christmas traditions from around the world. In many of the earlier years' catalogs, Hank Ketcham's famous comic strip troublemaker Dennis the Menace popped up throughout the book in specially drawn cartoon panels that commented on the merchandise on that particular page.

Beginning in 1970 and continuing for several years, Sears put Pooh not only in its catalogs and stores, but on television as well. The two Disney films that had been made up to that time, *Winnie the Pooh and the Honey Tree* (1966) and *Winnie the Pooh and the Blustery Day* (1968), were each the perfect length to fit a half-hour time slot, so they were presented as specials, with appropriate commercial interruptions from Sears. *Honey Tree* usually aired near the Easter clothes-buying season, while *Blustery Day* usually blew in during the week of, or just after, Thanksgiving. For that film's presentation, new opening animation was produced showing the Pooh crew busily hanging Christmas decorations on the Sears logo. At the close of the show, their job completed, Owl and Rabbit and the others left the screen, with Pooh taking a final moment to pull a cord and illuminate the wreath surrounding the logo. For youngsters such as this author, this small piece of animation was the surest sign yet that the big day was not far off.

Pooh and Dennis were not the only characters enlisted in the cause of Sears. In the early 1960s, the store made much of its snaring of a certain celebrity who was as well known for his reputation as an art connoisseur and gourmet cook as for his acting abilities. The 1964 catalog used this singular personage to promote its various Christmas departments, although the actor's name and reputation make the ad campaign sound somewhat odd in retrospect. To quote the blurb:

> Once again Sears has drawn upon the impeccable taste of Vincent Price. We now offer the same delicate ornaments, the same tree that Mr. Price selected and decorated in his own home.

Stop grinning and admit it: You are mentally picturing a withered, dead stick of a tree adorned with skulls and black widow spiders, complete with cobwebs instead of angel hair, aren't you? Although Vincent Price might be one of the last people any-

Sears introduced its collection of Winnie the Pooh toys, accessories, and children's clothing in 1965, anticipating the release of the first Pooh cartoon from Disney the following year.

Disney produced new animation of the Pooh crew for the openings and closings of the NBC telecasts of the films, which were sponsored by Sears just in time for Christmas.

one would think of to recommend their Christmas decorations, Sears was sincerely proud of its association with him. As an art critic, Price obtained original paintings of fabulous value to be distributed by Sears and loaned his name to a complete line of art supplies. Back in the world of Christmas, he also put his stamp of approval on certain Christmas cards and candies. (No, the cards did not say "Drop dead, Merry Christmas," and the candy did not turn one into a fanged fiend when eaten.)

That same 1964 catalog also devoted a page to the Vincent Price Movie Maker's Outfit, a home movie kit intended to improve consumers' 8-millimeter films. For $148.50, families that aspired to be the next Warner Brothers could get a camera, lighting, tripod, editing equipment, film, props, costumes, makeup, and the Vincent Price director's manual and scripts for three productions: *The Nativity*, *The Frog Prince*, and (it had to be there) *Dr. Psycho*. Just because Price was trying to show that he could be cultured as well as creepy, that did not mean he was going to turn his back on his day—or, make that night—job.

Along with the big-name catalogs, such as Sears, Montgomery Ward, and Spiegel, dozens of smaller companies sent out special catalogs devoted to Christmas merchandise. One of those was Spencer Gifts, which offered the infamous flat reindeer with footlights by promoting them as a gorgeous 3-D lawn display. Not all of Spencer's merchandise descriptions stretched the

Above: *Giant retailers such as Sears and Montgomery Ward were not the only ones to issue Christmas catalogs. Small, locally owned department stores did the same thing, and their covers were frequently works of art.* Right: *When thinking of celebrities to recommend decorations for their Christmas trees, Vincent Price would probably not be the first one to come to most people's minds.*

truth as widely as the one for those runt reindeer, but glancing through one of the vintage catalogs shows that artwork was used to illustrate items far more often than were actual photographs. Highly critical shoppers might have decided there must be a reason for that.

Some of Spencer's items were rather straightforward, if a bit on the cheap side. A set of seven plastic candy canes, each with its own bulb attached, would set you back $7.98 if you wanted to line the front walk with them. For 99 cents, you could get two sheets of cookie molds for producing edibles in the shape of a bell, star, tree, and Santa. Unfortunately, the pans, though described as "heavy duty aluminum," were closer to the consistency of aluminum foil, and the molds were so shallow that the cookies—when they did not burn during the baking process—were about as thick as saltine crackers. Spencer also offered door decorations, including a wreath with blinking red candle for $1 or, for those who wanted to splurge, a miniature evergreen with attached ornaments for $2.79. And we cannot forget such ever-popular products as a Santa suit for the family dog, toilet paper imprinted with Christmas cartoons in red and green ink, and soap molded into the shape of Santa's beaming face.

Speaking of that jolly old man, Spencer could deliver him to your home in multiple other forms. To decorate your front portal, you could order a Santa doorman made of

Left and above: ***Spencer Gifts may have specialized in somewhat inexpensive gift ideas, but at least it knew how to draw attention by putting an elf in leotards on the cover.*** **Below:** ***Spencer's cookie molds may have sounded like a good idea at the time, but just look how watery the dough would have to be in order to pour it into them.***

For ridiculously low prices, one could get a light-bedecked Santa for the front door or a stuffed one to sit on the front porch. Believe me, the stuffed one looked nowhere near this jolly and realistic.

lacquered paperboard, who "winked" at visitors by virtue of one eye being printed on a lenticular disk, much like the changing pictures common in boxes of Cracker Jack. (This one closed eye did give him some resemblance to Popeye the Santa Man.)

Another offering was a 5-foot, 5-inch plastic Santa that could be stuffed with paper to fill out his form. The illustration made him look appropriately jolly, but once the actual figure was set up on the porch, it looked rather like a petrified corpse. Perhaps Vincent Price was moonlighting by recommending products for Spencer.

A final Spencer item that remains in a class by itself was the personalized Santa record. First, the catalog description:

> Santa talks to your child and calls him by his first name! So thrilling as youngster plays the record! Santa really talks to him personally! And speaks to him about being good, his reindeer, etc. So exciting as child sings "Jingle Bells" with Santa and helpers. Each name individually recorded on unbreakable 78 rpm record.

Well, most of that was fairly accurate . . . But what the description did not say was that the whole record ran less than ninety seconds, and to make matters even worse, it was not even Santa who mentioned the child's name. After an opening chorus of "Jingle Bells," as promised, Santa arrives behind all eight (or was it nine?) reindeer, who give out a collective "brrrrrr" as Santa remarks, "That was a cold trip from the North Pole." To Spencer's credit, the actor who plays Santa did have a nearly perfect voice and inflection for the role; it is just unfortunate that he was not given more to do with it. After some more byplay with his squeaky-voiced helpers, the big moment comes when Santa announces, "And here's our first chimney! Whose chimney is this, my little elf?" That is the cue for what sounds for all the world like a bored teenager to switch on the microphone, fill in the blank with "______'s chimney, Santa Claus," then kill the mike with an audible click. Having been reminded of whose house he is visiting, Santa announces that he hopes the child has been good, because he has "lots of bright, new shiny toys" for him or her. He never does make it down the chimney before the record ends, but instead decides, "There are a lot of other chimneys to go down and a lot of other children to see," and bellowing, "Merry Christmas," he fades into the distance as the choir finishes "Jingle Bells." Oh well, so it was one of Santa's lesser helpers who actually said the kid's name. For a dollar, what would one expect, the Radio City Music Hall Rockettes?

Despite Spencer's claim, when the big moment came for the child's name to be spoken on this record, it was not by Santa himself, but by one of his minor helpers.

Many of the five-and-ten-cent stores—which became more accurately known as variety stores after their prices went up—issued Christmas booklets, but only some of them could be classified as catalogs. Woolworth's was such an American retail institution that advertising hardly seemed necessary, yet for a few years, a Woolworth's Christmas Book served dual purposes: It was a comic book with pages promoting the store's Christmas merchandise intertwined. The sales pages were not actually worked into the comic story, but they were hosted by the same cast of characters, in the tradition of contemporary children's television programs.

The 1952 Woolworth's book concerns itself with "Santa's Candy Rocket Ship," in which the bearded philanthropist takes three children, Betty, Billy, and their tagalong baby brother, Caboose, on a magical trip around the world, aided by the solid white Marsho the Marshmallow Bear. The story for 1953 is "Santa and the Snowball Patrol," introducing us to two more adventurous kids, Janie and Jimmie, and their wisecracking sidekick, Gabby the Parrot. After the youngsters' snowman comes to life (no, he isn't Frosty), he shows them how to roll in "magic flying snow" so they can head for the North Pole and join the Snowball Patrol in escorting Santa's sleigh. A lucky thing, too, because during his trip, Santa is attacked by the unfriendly, frozen natives of Cube Island, who have never heard of him. But the square-shaped ice people are won over by Santa's good nature and

Woolworth's early 1950s Christmas giveaway booklets deftly blended comic stories with pages in which the characters plugged the store's merchandise.

provide him with a bowl of candy ice cubes to distribute along with his toys.

One of Woolworth's competitors, W. T. Grant (they of the orange and blue storefronts), also issued Christmas books, but without the direct sales pitch of merchandise pages. Titles such as *Santa's Ride* (1959) and *The Little Tree That Wasn't Wanted* (1960) were presented not so much as comic books, but as illustrated text pieces. The only advertising for Grant's was on the exterior and interior covers. Other variety stores, including J. J. Newberry and G. C. Murphy, issued even more generic books, usually with the only clue to their origin being the store name printed on the back cover. Murphy's went just a step further, giving the following short poem:

Whether ornaments or Christmas cakes,
Candies, clothes or toys,
You'll find them all at Murphy's
For Mom, Pop, girls and boys.
So bring your list and start right in
To do your Christmas shopping.
You'll be surprised how fast you'll find
Grand gifts for every stocking!

***The W. T. Grant stores had a different giveaway booklet each Christmas. More than one person has noticed the similarity between the 1960 premium,* The Little Tree That Wasn't Wanted, *and the 1965* A Charlie Brown Christmas.**

Okay, so we've spent a lot of time browsing through the Christmas catalogs and picking out just what we'd like to have. Even that experience paled compared with a personal visit to one of the big stores, at least for those who lived within driving distance of one of them. Most of us baby boomers grew up in the suburbs, where variety stores were the most common, but somewhere nearby, there was always that remote fantasyland known as downtown, where the truly lavish department stores could be found. Neighborhoods and shopping malls were attractive enough during the Christmas season, but nothing was

Left: *The downtown area of any large city became a wonderland during the Christmas season. Indianapolis decorated its Market Square with an elaborate series of tableaux illustrating the first Christmas.* Right: *Most department stores had some sort of giveaway item that Santa Claus could pass out to keep the youngsters from going away empty-handed—and also to remind the kids and their parents to shop there.*

quite like what happened to the downtown shopping district during that approximately four-week period.

Like so many of our other childhood traditions, this custom went much further back in time than our own relatively recent existence. The huge department stores of New York City had begun the tradition of decorating their windows for Christmas in the 1870s. At first, said decorations primarily consisted of creative ways of displaying the merchandise that could be purchased therein. By the 1880s, though, a new concept was taking root. Improvements in mechanization meant that windows could now be decorated with elaborate moving figures and objects that not only served to draw attention to merchandise, but at times took its place completely. The unveiling of Macy's Christmas windows became an annual New York tradition.

New York was always the trendsetter when it came to window displays, and in fact, there were virtually no other cities with stores of the same magnitude. (Chicago, Philadelphia, and Los Angeles followed close behind but were still in the Big Apple's big shadow.) Smaller stores in the rest of the country contented themselves with displays more suited to their own financial ability. Those that could not afford gigantic animated scenery used simpler figures constructed of wood, or even cardboard, with motors behind them to give them some degree of movement. One memorable scene in

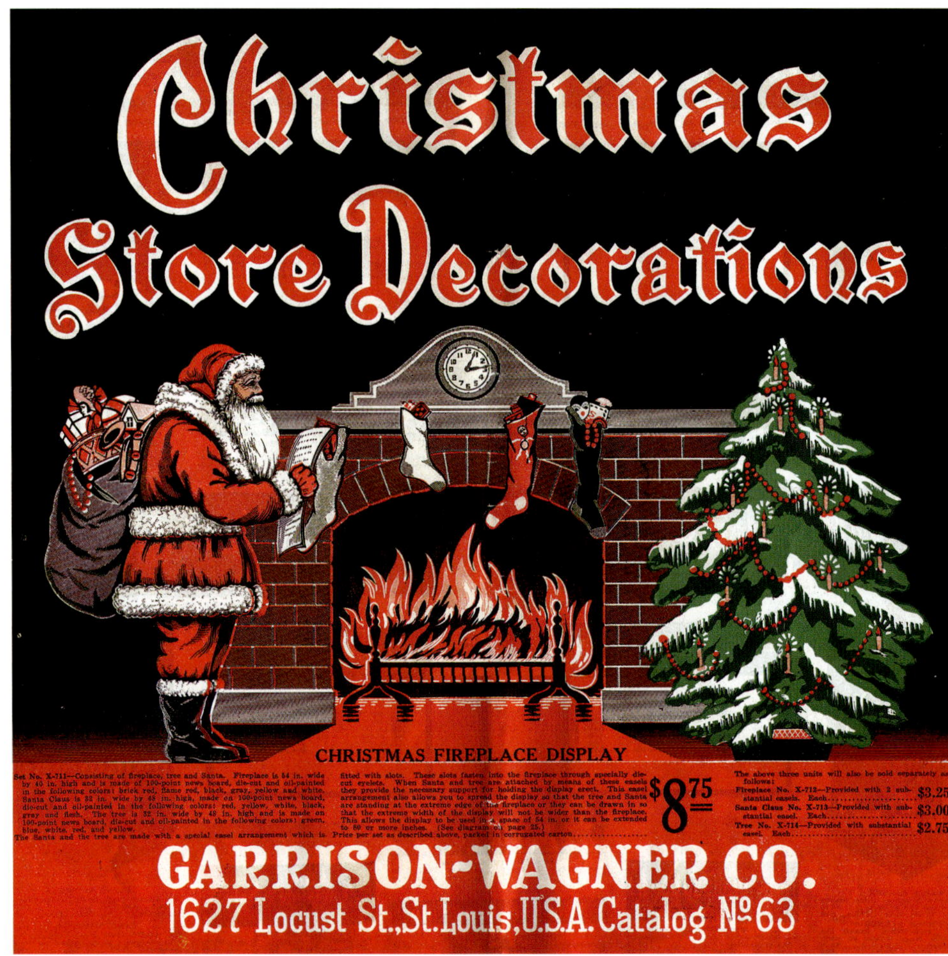

This 1928 catalog from the Garrison-Wagner Company is a terrific illustration of the state of Christmas store displays of that era.

Bob Hope's Christmas-themed movie *The Lemon Drop Kid* (1950) involves the comic, on the lam as usual, hiding in a department store window where a flat cutout Santa Claus mechanically bends forward and back again, handing a present to a mannequin dressed as an old lady. In an attempt to escape undetected, Hope hides behind the flat Santa and mimics the animated figure's movements, snatching pieces of the mannequin's attire one at a time. Once disguised as a grandma himself, Hope makes a quick exit, leaving the flat Santa giving gifts to a nude figure. Perhaps it is worth noting here that *The Lemon Drop Kid* also featured the debut of the song that would best come to embody the flavor of Christmas in a large city: "Silver Bells." It has become such a standard holiday tune that most people have forgotten it was originally written for Hope's streetwise character to sing in this film.

A window display of quite a different sort caused a sensation on New York's Fifth Avenue. Variety store tycoon S. H. Kress—yet another who entered the market that F. W. Woolworth had created—chose to spend large parts of his vast fortune on artwork, which he in turn bequeathed to various cities that did not already have their own art museums. The various S. H. Kress

One of the 1928 Garrison-Wagner displays was this two-dimensional Santa Claus that mechanically tipped his hat over and over again.

As stores grew larger and more elaborate, so did their holiday decorations. These giant ornaments and candy canes were made available for both department store main floors and the up-and-coming shopping malls.

Collections were the beginnings of such museums in many of those towns, but Kress was especially pleased with his 1938 purchase of the painting *Adoration of the Shepherds* by Giorgione. Then, as now, there were always those who wished that the religious aspect of Christmas could be kept more front and center than the commercial trappings, and Kress decided to do what he could about that. He displayed his valued (and valuable) *Adoration of the Shepherds* in the main window of the flagship Kress store at Fifth Avenue and 39th Street. The incongruity of a priceless work of art in a five-and-ten-cent store's window did not go without note. Kress historian Bernice Thomas quotes another writer, Kate Simon, as describing *Adoration of the Shepherds* as

"surrounded by spikes of cloth poinsettia, tinsel, tin angels and shining tree ornaments." Somewhat skeptically, Thomas reports that no photograph of the display has yet been located, so it is uncertain whether Simon was describing it from "personal recollection, hearsay, or imagination."

Since most storeowners did not have the income to purchase genuine Old Masters artwork for their windows, many different companies came into being to supply their needs. This meant that many of the same settings could be found in different stores in different cities, unlike the displays at Macy's and its ilk, which were custom-made for one store only. The mass-produced animated windows followed certain predictable patterns. Many of them were woodland scenes, with animated animals ranging from mice to penguins getting ready for the season. Another subset depicted Santa's workshop or other doings of the old man and his elves. There were scenes seemingly made entirely of candy, including the people, and others that replicated typical Currier and Ives–style winter settings in either the city or the country. No matter what the scenes were or where they were set up, they always drew a crowd that would stand around on the

Santa and his elves, with their animated antics, and the always-popular people made out of candy were two of the endless types of department store window displays.

This animated display appears to have taken more than a little inspiration from Disney's much-loved "It's a Small World" ride. Maybe these carolers are singing that catchy song.

sidewalk and gaze at the wonders behind the glass.

The crowds gathering in front of the stores gave quite a few retailers an even better idea that would help solve another problem common to the Christmas holidays. Who among you nostalgic readers could possibly forget being taken to one of the largest stores in your area to sit on Santa's lap and tell him what you wanted for Christmas? (Admittedly, it could be a bit upsetting when you ran into him in a different store later the same day, and he did not seem to remember your name or anything on your list.) Christmas historian Karal Ann Marling traced the tradition of the department store Santa back to 1890 and the Boston Store of Brockman, Massachusetts. However, department store expert Jan Whitaker dug deeper and found jolly old St. Nick hanging his stocking cap at Ridley's in New York City as far back as 1874. New York must have seemed like a second home to Santa in the late nineteenth century, as Whitaker states that he also loafed around Ehrich Brothers in 1880. Whitaker quotes a 1902 Macy's ad as claiming that year would mark Santa's forty-seventh visit to the store—but this could have been advertising hyperbole based on the number of Christmases the store had observed in its history, not a reference to the old gent's appearances in person.

Regardless of when Santa first made the trip, Marling and Whitaker agree that he did not really come to town to stay until the

1920s. From that point on, there was no prying him loose from his annual department store gig. The line of children waiting to talk to him could stretch through the aisles, blocking the paths of more profitable shoppers—and there was always the likely chance that the long wait would cause some kid to go berserk with boredom and start taking it out on his or her parents, other kids, or even (horrors!) Santa.

Those sidewalk window gazers proved to be the inspiration for at least one solution. Stores began to disguise the Santa waiting line by turning it into a walk-through attraction; this also served to get shoppers to come into the store rather than stay out on the sidewalk where they couldn't buy anything. These manufactured Christmas environments went by many different names, depending on the particular store; Santa Land was one moniker, while so many of them were called the Enchanted Forest that the term became a generic phrase in the amusement industry, describing any sort of walk-through attraction with animated figures.

Yes, the Enchanted Forests were loaded with the same types of animated scenes that graced the display windows, usually set up in a series of tableaux that provided interesting enough scenery to keep youngsters (and their parents) entertained during the wait for Santa's lap. In one grotto, the elves would be seen grooming the reindeer or busily making toys. (Maybe this came in handy when Mom or Dad had to explain why the toys under the Christmas tree bore price stickers from that store.) If the forest theme were to be well and truly employed, there was sure to be myriad animated animals, either humanized or in their natural state, frolicking under snow-covered branches.

Department store Santas were a highly anticipated part of the Christmas season for most kids, including this one. Yes, that is your beloved author getting up close and personal with St. Nick.

The walk-through world of Uncle Mistletoe, the Christmas symbol for Marshall Field's in Chicago, was known as Cozy Cloud Cottage, but other than the name, it sounds to have been much like its cousins in stores across the country. As evidence, we will now open our copies of the 1953 Uncle Mistletoe Little Golden Book, which describes the journey of siblings Peter and Bets as they set out for Cozy Cloud Cottage. See if author Jane Werner's text does not sound like a word-for-word description of what one would have seen in nearly any large store of that era:

> Through miles of those frosty woods they walked, on and on. Gold and green deer paused to watch them pass. Enchanted swans looked up at them from ponds as smooth as glass. . . . The sky was filled with a cloud, it seemed, of numberless bright balloons. Under each balloon hung

Color me A&S Santa Land

SIXTH FLOOR

SANTA

THIS MUST BE WHERE YOU GO IN!

ABRAHAM & STRAUS

EVERYTHING IS MOVING! WOW! THE FUNNY TEDDY BEAR IS SELLING FRESH GREENS!

GEE WHIZ! THE SNOW PEOPLE HAVE THEIR OWN BANDWAGON !!!

SEE THEM MAKING GINGERBREAD COOKIES!

LOOK AT THEM SELLING FRESH FISH! SEE THE FUNNY LOOKING WALRUS!

OOH! SEE THEM ON THEIR REINDEER CAROUSEL!

LOOK! THERE'S WHERE SANTA LIVES!

HO! HO! COME TELL SANTA WHAT YOU WANT FOR CHRISTMAS

HEY! LET'S GO UP TO THE 8TH FLOOR AND RIDE THE MERRY-GO-ROUND!

SEE! IT ONLY COSTS 29¢ AND WE GET A PRESENT, TOO!

SUCH A WONDERLAND AT A&S...WORTH A TRIP FROM ANYWHERE!

Left: *Stores devised ingenious ways to keep kids in the Santa waiting line from becoming bored. One of the most popular was to create an entire walk-through environment with animated figures in an ever-changing procession of scenes.* Above and facing page: *The store walk-through displays usually took the name of Santaland or, in many other cases, the Enchanted Forest. Most were basically the same, no matter what they were called.*

REGISTER
FOR A FREE 11-FT.
ANIMAL FAIR
'HENRY DOG"
Nothing to buy,
no obligation!
All youngsters
register in
Toyland, 6th Floor
downtown.
Drawing Dec. 23 . . .
King Henry will
be delivered to
winner Dec. 24!
OUR FOREST IS ENCHANTED!
AND SANTA'S WAITING! SIXTH FLOOR, DOWNTOWN
Where but in an enchanted forest could you have a chat with a Christmas Tree that
talks through big ruby red lips? Or watch a bear dance, an elephant jump, little people
made of candy whirl and twist? There's a happy surprise 'round every
bend of the magical snowy white forest, glistening with a "zillion" icicles and a "trillion"
twinkling fairy lights! All the lively forest inhabitants
knock themselves out to entertain, and Santa
waits at the fork in the road!
To bring your group or class call
252-0311, Ext. 276 for reservations
Pizitz

a basket filled with toys. . . . So Peter, Bets and Tony Pony hurried along through a forest of Christmas trees.

As the entire retail world changed in the 1970s and 1980s, individual store displays such as the Enchanted Forests were plowed under and their land reclaimed. In fact, most of the old downtown department stores died a slow and agonizing death as shoppers were lured into the malls that had taken the place of the former retail centers. Rather than each store in a mall having its own Santa, it was much easier (and less confusing) for the mall to set up a single jolly old gent in his own centrally located space. Even at that, the walk-through environment persisted on a smaller scale; in the late 1970s, the Disney studios licensed a set of animated versions of Mickey Mouse, Donald Duck, the Seven Dwarfs, and their Disneyland companions for a mall setup that was advertised under the brand name of Disney's Wonderful World of Christmas.

Although most of the downtown stores tossed their Christmas displays into the garbage once the demand was no longer there, occasionally one became enough of a local institution to warrant serious preservation. The Enchanted Forest of Goldsmith's store in Memphis, for example, lives on—at least in name, if not with the original fixtures—long after that store's demise by being set up in the city's Pink Palace Museum as a fund-raiser for the Le Bonheur Children's Medical Center. The Enchanted Christmas Village, a yearly fixture of Lit Brothers in Philadelphia, was eventually acquired by the Please Touch children's museum and also survives in that form. Most of the others have vanished as thoroughly as a snowflake in June.

While department stores were encouraging people to spend money in a blizzard of Christmas shopping, banks used this type of nostalgic artwork to remind everyone to begin saving for next year.

The Uncle Mistletoe Little Golden Book worked Marshall Field's own walk-through display into the story and the illustrations.

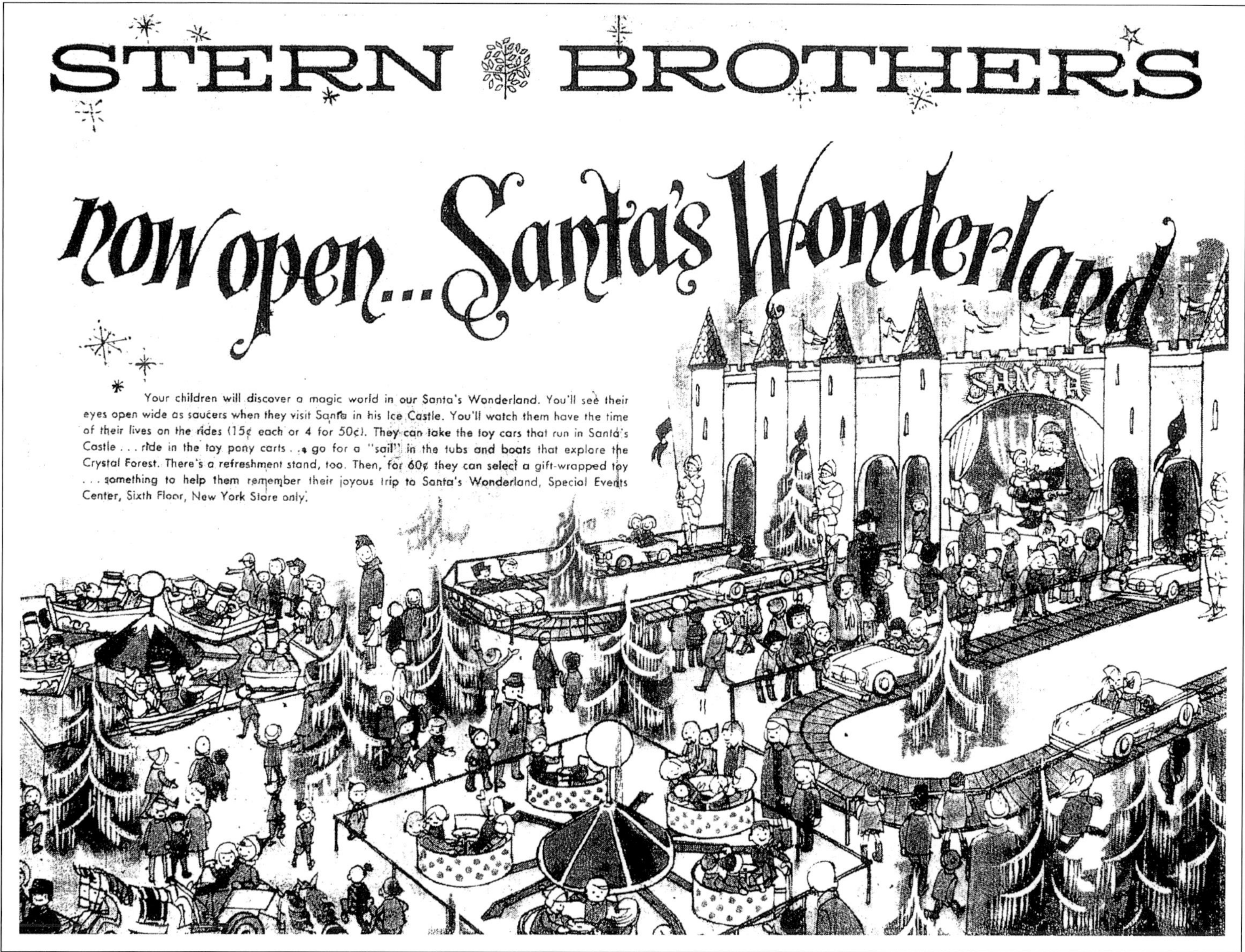

Some of the larger stores took the Santaland-Enchanted Forest concept to theme park extremes, with miniature trains and amusement rides that took up even more floor space.

Macy's also came up with a holiday promotion that eventually overshadowed even the company's legendary animated window displays. In 1924, a group of store employees got together to put on a parade through the streets of New York on Thanksgiving morning. Part of its intention was to promote the fact that Macy's had just opened a new addition to its huge building at Herald Square (Broadway and 34th Street), which would justifiably make the complex "the world's largest store." The appeal of Macy's Christmas Parade, as it was advertised, was so great that the event was turned into an annual one, under the more legendary name Macy's Thanksgiving Day Parade.

There was a living link between the parade and the famed Macy's Christmas windows. For many years, the look of both was the responsibility of artist and puppeteer Tony Sarg. Few people today are familiar with Sarg's name and work, but in those days, he was practically as well known as Jim Henson and the Muppets were a few generations later.

Sarg was already busy designing the annual animated window displays when his employer asked him to do something to help improve the parade. The first few processions had included caged animals borrowed from the Central Park Zoo, but since live beasts—especially after being pulled along city streets for miles—were generally not feeling the holiday spirit too well, their roars and growls were frightening children along the parade route. Sarg was charged with coming up with some invention that would replace the cranky live animals. Using his puppeteering skills as a starting point, Sarg designed large rubber balloons that, once inflated with helium, could be manipulated from underneath by a system of ropes, much as a marionette is controlled from above. Once the new Macy's balloons debuted in 1927, there was no turning back.

Plenty of other volumes describe the history of this national institution from that point onward; this book is mainly concerned with its role in the larger scheme of Christmas. The Macy's parade remained a local New York event throughout the remainder of the 1920s, 1930s, and most of the 1940s, minus the period of 1942–44, when it was suspended during wartime. The rest of the country really did not think much about it, at this point, except when short film clips of the procession made it into the weekly newsreel at the theater. The nation's movie houses were again responsible for what little non-New Yorkers knew about the parade when 20th Century Fox released *Miracle on 34th Street* during the summer (yes, summer!) of 1947. The film contained footage that was shot on location during the 1946 parade, giving everyone at least a glimpse of what was going on in the Big Apple.

Accounts differ as to just what year the Macy's parade was first televised nationally, but at least by 1953, it was on its way to becoming a big TV event. As the number of local stations and network affiliates grew, the annual telecast reached a larger audience every Thanksgiving morning. Most baby boomers remember the parade best during the late 1950s and 1960s, when the giant balloon effigies of Popeye, Bullwinkle, Donald Duck, Linus the Lionhearted, Underdog, Sinclair's Dino the Dinosaur, Smokey the Bear, the Happy Dragon, and many

Once the Macy's Thanksgiving Day Parade had become an annual television event, it came to represent the start of the holiday season to viewers nationwide.

When the heroic Underdog joined the Macy's balloon cast in 1964, the store also handed out these records cementing its association with the crime-fighting canine. BILL SMITH

other friends could be counted on to appear. The parade also included floats promoting current and upcoming movie releases, marching bands that could be from your own hometown—and bringing up the rear on the final float, jolly old St. Nicholas himself, officially ushering in the Christmas shopping season.

For anyone who cares to notice, the parade is still there for all to enjoy today. Oh sure, the cartoon character balloons are different, appealing to today's kids' tastes rather than the antiquated taste buds of their elders. The stars on the floats may well be people you and I have never heard of. But Santa still makes his annual appearance at the end, and it still gives one a tingle of excitement to see him, even though most malls have welcomed the busy old gent for at least two weekends by the time Thanksgiving Day arrives. When Kris Kringle (as he was alternately known in *Miracle on 34th Street*) stops in front of Macy's Herald Square entrance bay, it is easy to believe that the holiday season has finally and officially arrived.

For years, Macy's parade managed to get along with no visible corporate logos other than the sponsoring department store's. That changed in 1965. The McDonald's corporation had decided to get into national advertising, after ten years of relying on its regional offices to promote the red-and-white-striped drive-ins of their own areas. The company was offered a deal it couldn't refuse to include its first network television commercials in NBC's broadcast of the 1965 Macy's parade. McDonald's chose this momentous event in its history to introduce to the nation a character who had previously been known only in the Washington, D.C., area: that kooky clown of the condiment continent, Ronald McDonald.

Not only would Ronald be seen coast to coast in the commercials, but some of the creative chefs behind the golden arches cooked up a way to get him into the line of march. A high school band from Pennsylvania was scheduled to perform during the parade but had been unable to raise the money for the trip. McDonald's agreed to sponsor the band if the uniforms could be modified to include the company symbol: the arches with a slash line through them, representing the restaurant's slanted roof. The company then found the "world's largest bass drum," a leftover from the University of Texas, and refitted it with the McDonald's logo on the side. The drum was rolled down the parade route, with good

The McDonald's All-American High School Band, under the baton of Radio City Music Hall director Paul Lavalle, was an annual part of the Macy's parade for many years.

By the time of this 1966 ad, the Macy's balloon cast had inflated to include the figures that became the most familiar to baby boomers.

old Ronald—or make that *new* Ronald—beating it all the way. Despite Macy's protests at McDonald's expanding its paid commercials into the content of the parade, the event brought fast-food advertising to television and linked it to an unlikely association with Christmas.

McDonald's continued its connections with both Macy's and the holiday season in future years. After the initial Pennsylvania band and Ronald's debut, McDonald's formed the All-American High School Band, under the baton of Radio City Music Hall director Paul Lavalle. Two outstanding musicians were chosen from each of the fifty United States and massed together to form a "best of the best" aggregation. McDonald's even issued a small long-playing record of some of the band's performances, with Macy's parade photos on the front and back covers. The recording of the band's songs proves that McDonald's had found one more way to sneak in a commercial plug where it was not expected. One of their selections was the old spiritual "Down by the Riverside," which had recently received new lyrics to become the theme song for the McDonald's commercials: "McDonald's is your kind of place / It's such a happy place / Such a hap-hap-happy place . . ."

Once other fast-food chains saw what McDonald's had done with the Christmas season, they decided to get into the spirit too. Unlike hamburgers and milkshakes, Kentucky Fried Chicken could at least be considered a reasonable menu item for a Christmas dinner—as long as the family did not have its heart set on said dinner being home-cooked—so the poultry pluckers took out magazine ads to promote the idea of bringing their product home for the holidays. Going even further than that, for several years KFC offered LPs with such titles as "Christmas Eve with Colonel Sanders"; the selections were past Christmas hits from the RCA library, but the covers always featured new photography or artwork to show the genial white-suited Colonel in his own brand of Christmas celebrations.

After using Macy's to establish itself during the Christmas season, McDonald's embraced the holiday in a big way. But wait—if the Hamburglar is giving police officer Big Mac a hamburger as a gift, does that mean Big Mac is a cannibal?

Fast-food restaurants were just discovering Christmas during the 1960s, but those promoting other products had known of the holiday's selling potential for many years. The proliferation of ads, both broadcast and print, during the Christmas season got under many people's skin, and recording artist Stan Freberg aimed one of his most pointed satirical records at this trend. "Green Chritma" managed to offend nearly everyone, from the advertisers whose methods he skewered to pious types who simply objected to the dollar signs in the title without hearing what the record was all about.

In his autobiography, Freberg admitted that even with his dander up, he was not saying that all types of Christmas advertising were equal offenders: "I have no quarrel with companies advertising children's toys under Christmas trees, or facial cosmetics, or books, or cassette tapes, or luggage, or clothes to wear—things one might normally give as presents to one's family or friends." Certain ads that really stretched credibility when tying their products to Christmas were what made his wickedly satirical mind kick into gear. "What finally sent me into action was a magazine ad showing a family coming down in their pajamas and robes on Christmas morning," he said. "As the mother, children and dog look on in wonder, the father hovers back a bit on the stairs, a proud look on his face. There, under the tree, is a brand new set of five tubeless tires. . . . Good tires on a car are very important. But talk to me about that during the other eleven months of the year, okay?" Freberg also cited a magazine ad for Jell-O that featured a Christmas tree with packages of the flavored gelatin dangling from the branches, in lieu of any other ornaments. It was too much for him to take.

To describe "Green Chritma" briefly, it involves the ad agency run by Mr. Scrooge

Through magazine ads and giveaway record albums, Kentucky Fried Chicken made sure that all of its patrons could enjoy a finger-lickin' Christmas.

(Freberg), where the sleazy account executives are planning thinly disguised campaigns for Coca-Cola and Lucky Strike cigarettes. The only reasonable rhetoric comes from Bob Cratchit (cartoon actor Daws Butler, speaking in his natural voice), who tries to interrupt with logic. His pleas are drowned out by Scrooge playing noisy commercials: "Say, mother, as sure as there's an X in Christmas, you can be sure those are Tiny Tim chestnuts roasting!" Finally, Cratchit can stand it no longer:

CRATCHIT: Don't you realize, Christmas has a significance . . . a meaning!
SCROOGE: A sales curve! Wake up, Cratchit, it's later than you think.
CRATCHIT: (sadly) I know, Mr. Scrooge . . . I know.

The record ends with a loud chorus:

On the first day of Christmas, the advertising's there
With newspaper ads
Billboards too
Business Christmas cards
And commercials on a pear tree!

The final sound is "Jingle Bells" played on a cash register. The whole thing greatly upset the radio stations whose disc jockeys were supposed to play it. Sponsors insisted that their commercials not be aired within fifteen minutes of "Green Chritma," because it voided the very sales messages they were trying to push. Ironically, soon after being lambasted in the record, Coca-Cola came to Freberg to enlist his services for a new ad campaign!

With all the commotion caused by Freberg's record, everyone forgot (or never knew) that in the vastly different world of 1941, author Harry Irving Phillips had made a similar comment on Christmas advertising. In a spoof of "The Night before Christmas," Phillips cast Santa as a radio entertainer who

inserted messages from his sponsors between the lines of the poem:

He sprang to his team, cracked his whip
o'er his pets,
Saying, "All these eight reindeer smoke
Blank cigarettes."
Then I heard him exclaim as he drove
out of sight,
"Merry Christmas to all, and to all a
good night,
By arrangement with Rosenberg, Plotz
& Maloney,
The world-famous makers of Splendid
Baloney!"

Although commercials could cause a certain amount of holiday burnout, if not pure outrage, some became an anticipated part of the season through their creativity or sheer longevity. Norelco first featured a stop-motion animated Santa riding over the snow atop one of its electric razors in 1961. The commercial was updated several times, most recently in 1992, by which time Santa was animated by a computer rather than the painstaking frame-by-frame movement of stop motion. During the 1960s, it was so similar to the look of the Rankin/Bass specials that many people thought it had originally been created to air along with those

Some people believe that spelling "Christmas" as "Xmas" is a fairly recent sacrilegious custom. But take a look at this selection of banners being offered by Garrison-Wagner in 1928.

The Norelco Santa evolved from his original black and white stop-motion animated form of the 1960s to a computer-generated image in the early 1990s.

While General Electric was sponsoring the annual **Rudolph the Red-Nosed Reindeer** *telecast, the company conscripted the characters to plug its holiday gift ideas in magazine ads.*

shows. In fact, Rankin/Bass did animate special commercials for General Electric to be included with the original network broadcasts of *Rudolph the Red-Nosed Reindeer*. They featured the somewhat bumbling elves from that show, but not Rudolph, Santa, or the other star characters.

Coca-Cola mostly confined Santa to its print advertising. The company had made a big impression on everyone with its 1971 commercial featuring young people from around the world, gathered on a hilltop to deliver the anthem "I'd Like to Teach the World to Sing." This song did the almost unthinkable by breaking loose from its commercial origins to become a major success in its own right; I guess you could say it went from being a soft-drink jingle to a *pop* hit. For Christmas, Coke assembled a new group of international youths and had them stand in the shape of a Christmas tree, each participant holding a lighted candle. The lyrics of the song remained the same but were accompanied by bells in the background.

One of Coke's competitors, 7-Up, promoted itself as the Uncola, and its Christmas commercials featured a puppet rendition of an Undeer, with a voice by cartoon great Paul Frees. Puppets had plugged a different type of beverage in the early 1960s, when up-and-coming Muppeteer Jim Henson had created a long series of TV spots for various local coffee companies across the country. Any brand name could be inserted into the scripts, which were so short that they had little time for anything but a setup and a punch line. Each spot starred a happy character (whose voice sounded much like the one Henson later gave Kermit the Frog) and

Before we go, let's take one more look at some of those magnificent covers local stores used for their Christmas catalogs.

a grouchy one, who hated the sponsor's product. The pair's Christmas greeting featured the happy one dressed as Santa in a sleigh, with the grumpy one wearing reindeer antlers:

> HAPPY: Merry Christmas! It's a joy to serve ______ coffee to all you folks at Christmas time!
>
> GROUCHY: It's a joy for you—YOU'RE not havin' to pull the sled!

The Colorburst camera, Kodak's short-lived and ill-fated (read: patent-infringing) attempt to muscle in on Polaroid's exclusive turf of instant photographs, had a heartwarming spot. In the commercial, a young boy (Arnold) uses the Colorburst's in-a-minute technology to prove to his skeptical older brother (Joey) that a certain white-bearded old man in a red suit is in their living room at that very moment.

Another memorable ad was a typically emotional production by those sentinels of sentiment, Hallmark cards. A little girl is busily crayoning a picture of Santa for her dad, whom we see downstairs giving his wife a perfunctory good-bye kiss as he rushes to leave for work. The girl approaches him with her prized drawing, but he dismisses it with a flourish as he runs to make his business meeting. That night, passing by her room, he overhears her apparently talking to Santa Claus and enumerating the various toys she would like to have—and when she finishes, "But most of all, I want my Daddy," you'd think a spear had been run clean through him. Even for those of us who do not have children, Hallmark's little masterpiece reminds everyone that there are few areas where your life can have half as much influence as on a young mind.

EPILOGUE
Silent Night

Now, after all the weeks of frantic hoopla and advertising and assorted other forms of ballyhoo, it comes down to this. It is nighttime on Christmas Eve. The stores are all closed; everything that is going to be sold for this season has been sold; the employees have gone home to be with their loved ones. The traffic on the highways gradually diminishes, until no automobile headlights can be seen in either direction. Inside the houses, children are finally exhausted by their own excitement and have been put to bed. Their parents, nearly as exhausted from all that had to be done to get the house ready for visitors the next day, stumble off to bed as well. Seemingly the whole world is quiet . . . peaceful . . . as if waiting for something.

Surely there must be something appropriate I can say to wrap up this journey through what the Christmas season meant to baby boomers. Let's see: "Although it's been said, many times, many ways, merry Christmas to you." No, that's already been taken. What about "Merry Christmas to all, and to all a good night"? No, someone said that before too. Let's try "God bless us, every one." What, you mean that one's been used as well? How, then, can I put a bow on this package?

Ahhh, reliable old Cricket Records! On the back cover of one of Cricket's early 1960s Christmas LPs, an unidentified writer did an eloquent job of summing up the flavor of this moment. If I can't come up with something original, at least I can use something obscure enough that hardly anyone will have heard it before. Relax, and listen to this:

Christmas—a time of love. A time to remember our loved ones far away. The time to raise your voice in praise of the birth of Christ, our Savior. The time of year brotherly love becomes reality as strangers muffled against wintry blasts, and staggering beneath tinseled packages, say to each other, "Merry Christmas!"

Christmas—a time for children. Boys and girls nestled down in dreaming warmth on Christmas Eve, listening for the sounds of reindeer on the roof and Santa coming down the chimney. The laughter beneath the tree as their dreams come true on Christmas morn.

Christmas—a time of celebration. Trim the tree with bells, stars and candles, deck the halls with boughs of holly. It's the season to be jolly. Eager little hands place cherubs on the lower branches of the tree as the adults place the glowing star on top. A wonderland of lights blink down upon a rainbow of gift packages sleeping till Christmas morn.

Now, what more could I possibly add to that? Nothing, actually. So, as the Disney Christmas theme song put it, "from all of us to all of you," I hope this year is your merriest Christmas ever!

"A MERRY CHRISTMAS TO ALL," said Charlie Brown.

Bibliography

Bird, William L., Jr. *Holidays on Display*. New York: Princeton Architectural Press, 2007.

Brenner, Robert. *Christmas: 1960–Present*. Atglen, PA: Schiffer Books, 2002.

Chris, Teresa. *The Story of Santa Claus*. Secaucus, NJ: Chartwell Books, 1992.

Del Pozzo, Ralph, and David High. *Christmasland: ReCollections*. New York: Collins Design, 2006.

Eckstein, Bob. *The History of the Snowman*. New York: Simon Spotlight Entertainment, 2007.

Freberg, Stan. *It Only Hurts When I Laugh*. New York: Times Books, 1988.

Gardner, Martin. *The Annotated Night before Christmas*. New York: Summit Books, 1991.

Grippo, Robert M., and Christopher Hoskins. *Macy's Thanksgiving Day Parade*. Charleston, SC: Arcadia Publishing, 2004.

Hollis, Tim. *Hi There, Boys and Girls! America's Local Children's TV Programs*. Jackson, MS: University Press of Mississippi, 2001.

Hollis, Tim, and Greg Ehrbar. *Mouse Tracks: The Story of Walt Disney Records*. Jackson, MS: University Press of Mississippi, 2006.

Krasnow, Judy Gail. *Rudolph, Frosty and Captain Kangaroo: The Musical Life of Hecky Krasnow*. Santa Monica, CA: Santa Monica Press, 2007.

Lederman, Robert P. *Christmas on State Street*. Charleston, SC: Arcadia Publishing, 2002.

Love, John F. *McDonald's: Behind the Arches*. New York: Bantam Books, 1986.

Madden, Steven. *America's Parade: A Celebration of Macy's Thanksgiving Day Parade*. New York: Time Inc. Home Entertainment, 2001.

Marling, Karal Ann. *Merry Christmas! Celebrating America's Greatest Holiday*. Cambridge, MA: Harvard University Press, 2000.

Mendelson, Lee. *A Charlie Brown Christmas: The Making of a Tradition*. New York: HarperCollins, 2000.

Menendez, Albert J., and Shirley C. Menendez. *Christmas Songs Made in America*. Nashville, TN: Cumberland House, 1999.

Merck, Robert M. *Deck the Halls: Treasures of Christmas Past*. New York: Abbeville Press, 1992.

Rich, Mark. *100 Greatest Baby Boomer Toys*. Iola, WI: Krause Publications, 2000.

Richliano, James Adam. *Angels We Have Heard: The Christmas Song Stories*. Chatham, NY: Star of Bethlehem Books, 2002.

Smith, Lissa, and Dick Smith. *Christmas Collectibles*. Secaucus, NJ: Chartwell Books, 1993.

Smith, Travis. *Kitschmasland! Christmas Décor from the 1950s to the 1970s*. Atglen, PA: Schiffer Publishing, 2005.

Waggoner, Susan. *It's a Wonderful Christmas*. New York: Stewart, Tabori and Chang, 2004.

———. *Under the Tree*. New York: Stewart, Tabori and Chang, 2007.

Whitaker, Jan. *Service and Style: How the American Department Store Fashioned the Middle Class*. New York: St. Martin's Press, 2006.

Index

Page numbers in **bold** *refer to illustrations.*

SPARKLE
Christmas
SNOW

Christmas Nativity Set
The Story of
The First Christmas
In Colorful Cut-Out Scenes
And Life-Like Figures

Speaking for Everyone in Television . . .
TV GUIDE wishes you
a truly Merry Christmas